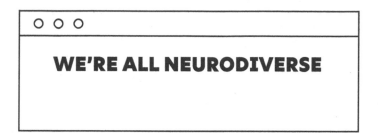

WE'RE ALL NEURODIVERSE

WE'RE ALL NEURODIVERSE

How to Build a Neurodiversity-Affirming
Future and Challenge Neuronormativity

SONNY JANE WISE

Jessica Kingsley Publishers
London and Philadelphia

First published in Great Britain in 2024 by Jessica Kingsley Publishers
An imprint of John Murray Press

1

Copyright © Sonny Jane Wise 2024

The right of Sonny Jane Wise to be identified as the Author of the Work has been asserted by them in accordance with the Copyright, Designs and Patents Act 1988.

Content warning: This book mentions racism.

A CIP catalogue record for this title is available from the British Library and the Library of Congress

ISBN 978 1 83997 578 3
eISBN 978 1 83997 579 0

Printed and bound in Great Britain by Clays Ltd

Jessica Kingsley Publishers' policy is to use papers that are natural, renewable and recyclable products and made from wood grown in sustainable forests. The logging and manufacturing processes are expected to conform to the environmental regulations of the country of origin.

Jessica Kingsley Publishers
Carmelite House
50 Victoria Embankment
London EC4Y 0DZ

www.jkp.com

John Murray Press
Part of Hodder & Stoughton Limited
An Hachette UK Company

Contents

CHAPTER 1

Introduction

You might be wondering why this book is called *We're All Neu-rodiverse*. It's because we are all a part of neurodiversity – neurodivergent and neurotypical alike. In order to understand why I wrote this book and why neurodiversity, neurodivergence and the Neurodiversity Paradigm are so important to me, I want to share a bit about my own lived experience.

I'm multiply neurodivergent, which means I diverge in many, many ways. In fact, I would probably say that every part of me diverges, from the way I think and feel to the way I learn and communicate. I was diagnosed with Autism and attention deficit hyperactivity disorder (ADHD) when I was only a child; as an adult, I was later diagnosed with bipolar disorder and borderline personality disorder (BPD).

I grew up believing there was something wrong with me. I grew up being told there was something wrong with me by teachers, professionals and family. I even received the same message from the kids around me, and while they may not have said it explicitly, it was reinforced in how they would bully me and exclude me. I was 11 years old when I tried to overdose on my medication for the first time, and it was because I thought if I took enough medication,

I would be fixed and everything would be better; I would be better. It was the logic of an 11-year-old who was told that medication makes me better.

I grew up hating myself. I hated myself as a child, I hated myself as a teenager and I hated myself throughout most of my 20s. I'm 30 years old now and I've spent more of my life hating myself than I have loving myself. When you hate yourself, you're not kind to yourself, you don't look after yourself, you don't reach out for help, you don't reach out for support, you don't surround yourself with people who accept you and love you. I grew up believing I was the problem and I needed to be fixed. Growing up believing all of that shaped how I viewed myself, it shaped my relationship with myself and it even shaped my relationships with other people. I thought I was undeserving of any kindness or love that came my way, because how on earth could someone like me if I was a broken mess? I never want to hate myself again. I don't want any other person to live their life hating themselves. I don't want anyone to hate themselves for their differences, for who they are.

I stopped feeling as though I was broken when I discovered the term 'neurodivergent'. I stopped feeling so alone when I discovered the neurodivergent community. I stopped hating myself and started accepting myself when I discovered the concept of neurodiversity. I stopped viewing myself as the problem and started recognizing the way society isn't set up to accommodate my differences or honour my needs when I discovered the concept of neurodiversity.

When I stopped viewing myself through the lens of the Pathology Paradigm and started viewing myself through the lens of the Neurodiversity Paradigm, it changed everything for me; it gave me a framework to begin to accept myself. I want that for others, I want that for everyone. I want individuals to accept their differences, I want parents to accept their children and teach them to embrace their differences, and I want mental health providers to support individuals and their differences rather than the default of fixing their differences. I want society to recognize and accept the diversity of existing, of functioning, of being human. It's why I believe the concept of neurodiversity and neurodivergence is so important and powerful because it's a framework that teaches individuals as well as society to accept our differences, compared to our current framework which frames our differences as a problem, a flaw, an abnormality and a disorder.

I want everyone to have the opportunity to understand themselves through the Neurodiversity Paradigm rather than the Pathology Paradigm. I want everyone to have the opportunity to recognize themselves as neurodivergent instead of disordered. I want everyone to know they belong to a community that accepts them and embraces them, because whenever I talk about neurodivergence online, I still get so many individuals telling me they didn't know they could identify as neurodivergent. They didn't know they *were* neurodivergent; they just thought they were broken, abnormal or unwell.

It's why I wanted to write this book; I realized there have been misunderstandings and misconceptions of the history and meaning of the terms 'neurodiversity' and 'neurodivergence'. Even though society is becoming more familiar with neurodiversity and neurodivergence, it's still only focusing on neurodivergences such as Autism and ADHD while other neurodivergences like bipolar and schizophrenia are commonly left out of the narrative.

It reminds me of the telephone game where someone thinks of a phrase and whispers it once into the next player's ear. That listener then has to try to correctly repeat that same phrase into the next player's ear and each player in the game has to do the same thing till the end. More often than not, the phrase has changed and the last person has heard something completely different. I feel as if that's what has happened with the term 'neurodivergent'; the meaning has changed compared to what the creator has whispered into our ears, figuratively speaking. I mean, even certifiable sources such as dictionaries don't have the correct definition of neurodivergent, which means it's difficult for individuals to even find the correct definition.

I wanted to write this book because I don't want individuals to be left out of the narrative. I don't want individuals to feel as though they aren't a part of the neurodivergent community, I don't want individuals to feel like the Neurodiversity Paradigm isn't for them. I do not believe anyone is inherently pathological; I do not believe anyone is broken or wrong for existing or functioning the way they do. I know what it feels like to grow up believing you're abnormal, wrong or broken, and I don't want anyone to view themselves that way. I also genuinely believe that we don't need to label people with a disorder in order to support their well-being. I think it's actually counterproductive, especially when disorder invokes feelings of shame, and shame is not a motivating factor when it comes to healing, recovering or looking after ourselves. It's why I'm so passionate about the Neurodiversity Paradigm because it isn't just a paradigm or lens for therapists and mental health providers to understand and support neurodivergent individuals but a paradigm and lens for society itself.

I want people to know they're included under the neurodivergent umbrella, and I want people to know they aren't disordered. I believe in the Neurodiversity Paradigm; I want more people to believe in the Neurodiversity Paradigm, and I want more people to view individuals using the lens of neurodiversity. I believe it will make a difference in how neurodivergent individuals understand themselves, and I believe it will make a difference in how providers and society support neurodivergent individuals. I think it's one of the most impactful things we can do – accepting ourselves and teaching others to accept ourselves. I see neurodiversity as the pathway to accepting our differences, honouring our needs and embracing who we are. I believe we are moving towards a more neurodiversity-affirming future, but in order to include everyone in that future, we need to be clear on what neurodiversity, neurodivergence and the Neurodiversity Paradigm mean. I feel so honoured to write this book, and I genuinely hope I have done this movement and this paradigm the justice it deserves.

Material marked with ⬇ can be downloaded from www.jkp.com/catalogue/book/9781839975783

CHAPTER 2

Key Definitions

I wanted to make sure this book could serve to support society's understanding and learning of neurodiversity and neurodivergence, which is why I knew I needed to make this book as accessible as possible. Where a lot of books often go wrong, I think, is that they assume the reader already has an understanding of any terms mentioned, but this time I want to make sure every reader is on the same page, which is why I've included a list of common terms you'll find throughout this book. You might already know these terms and that's okay. You're welcome to skip forward, but you're also welcome to continue to read this chapter to refresh your memory. See what the fuss is about, you know?

AAC

AAC stands for augmentative and alternative communication, which includes other forms of communication outside of oral speech.

Abolition

Abolition is a verb and a practice that refers to the act of getting rid of harmful systems and institutions that rely on punishment and control.

Ableism

Ableism is a system of oppression that disadvantages and discriminates against disabled people based on a set of assumptions that disabled people are less than, while non-disabled people are superior.

AFAB/AMAB

These are acronyms meaning assigned female at birth and assigned male at birth.

Alexithymia

Alexithymia is a common experience for neurodivergent individuals that refers to an inability or difficulty in identifying and describing emotions. Alexithymia has been described as lacking a label maker in your brain that tells you what emotion you're feeling.

Alter

Alter is common term used alongside headmate to describe someone within a system.

Autistic meltdowns

Meltdowns are an intense emotional and physical reaction that is often due to a combination of factors which can include masking, socializing, sudden changes, sensory and cognitive overload, and too many demands and expectations.

Burnout

Burnout is a state of physical and mental exhaustion that is often accompanied by a loss of skills and an inability to mask. Burnout is a common experience for neurodivergent individuals due to living in a neuronormative society with neuronormative expectations and demands as well as a lack of accommodations and resources.

Biological sex

Biological sex refers to our anatomy as male, female or intersex, and it includes our internal and external sex organs, chromosomes and hormones. It is important to remember that our biological sex is separate from our gender.

Cisnormativity

Cisnormativity is the assumption that all individuals have a gender identity that corresponds with the sex they were born as. It reinforces the gender binary and implies that cisgender is the default, normal gender. Cisnormativity is about making cisgender the societal norm, which privileges cisgender people over other people who diverge from this societal norm.

Discrimination

Discrimination is the unfair and unjust treatment of an individual based on identities or characteristics including race, gender, disability, neurodivergence, class and more.

DSM

The *Diagnostic and Statistical Manual of Mental Disorders* (DSM) is a handbook used by mental health professionals that provides a framework to categorize and diagnose disorders.

Gender

Gender is a set of socially constructed roles, characteristics, attributes and behaviours that society assigns to individuals.

Heteronormativity

Heteronormativity is the assumption that everyone is heterosexual and that heterosexuality is superior to all other sexualities, which results in labelling heterosexuality as the norm and other sexualities as abnormal. Heteronormativity is about making straight identities the societal norm, which privileges straight people over other people who diverge from this societal norm.

Hyperfocusing

Hyperfocusing is a specific state of focusing that allows an individual to be intensely focused for a long period of time.

Hypersensitivity

Hypersensitivity is an over-responsiveness to sensory input, where we often experience distress, discomfort or sensory overload from sensory input and we tend to require frequent breaks from sensory input. Neurodivergent individuals can experience hypersensitivity with one, some or all of the senses.

Hyposensitivity

Hyposensitivity is an under-responsiveness to sensory input where individuals often struggle to register low levels of sensory input or may receive less information from the senses. Individuals who are hyposensitive tend to seek out and need higher levels of sensory input and stimulation. Neurodivergent individuals can experience hyposensitivity with one, some or all of the senses.

Intersectionality

Intersectionality is a concept, developed by Kimberlé Crenshaw,[1] to understand how various identities and experiences in regard to race, culture, gender, sexuality, disability and neurodivergence

1   Kimberlé Crenshaw, 'Demarginalizing the Intersection of Race and Sex: A Black Feminist Critique of Antidiscrimination Doctrine, Feminist Theory, and Antiracist Politics [1989]', in *Feminist Legal Theory: Readings in Law and Gender*, ed. Katherine Bartlett (New York: Routledge, 2019), 57–80. https://doi.org/10.4324/9780429500480-5

come together and overlap to create a unique experience of discrimination, oppression and privilege. Intersectionality is a lens for viewing how inequality and power intersect with and exacerbate each other.

Interoception

Interoception is one of our senses that is responsible for our internal body awareness – our ability to feel and interpret our internal body signals such as hunger, thirst and pain.

Masking

Masking is the act or process of suppressing or hiding your traits, natural behaviours and responses while adopting alternative traits and behaviours in order to fit in, survive, cope and meet expectations.

Medical model of disability

The medical model of disability believes that disabled people are broken and disabled by whatever is wrong with their body or mind. According to the medical model, disabled people are in need of fixing in order to make them like everybody else.

Neurodiversity

Neurodiversity refers to the variability of human minds and all the unique and different ways that people can exist, think, act, process, feel and function. Neurodiversity refers to all human minds on the planet. It includes everyone – neurotypical and neurodivergent alike. It is simply a fact that the human population is diverse in our minds just as we are diverse in our ethnicity, gender, sexuality and physical ability.

Judy Singer was the first individual to use and develop neurodiversity in academia.[2] I would be doing a disservice to the Autistic community if I didn't acknowledge that neurodiversity actually first emerged as a term on email mailing lists in the early 1990s between Autistic adults, advocates and activists. Judy introduced it in her thesis where her primary mission was to recognize neurodiversity as another form of diversity and an important addition to intersectionality.

Neurodiverse

Neurodiverse is a term to describe a group of individuals who represent the spectrum of neurodiversity, which includes both neurotypical and neurodivergent individuals. Neurodiverse and neurodivergent are not interchangeable terms that mean the same thing. There is no such thing as a 'neurodiverse' person, because a single individual cannot be neurodiverse. We are all neurodiverse – society is neurodiverse, the entire human population is neurodiverse. When we use neurodiverse when we mean neurodivergent, we're actually implying that neurotypical people are not a part of neurodiversity. Let me put it this way: if you wouldn't want a neurotypical person calling themselves neurodiverse, it means that's not the word for you. The word you're looking for is neurodivergent.

Neurodivergent

Neurodivergent is an umbrella term to describe individuals whose mind or functioning falls outside dominant societal norms. It is an umbrella term that includes innate or genetic conditions as well as acquired or developed conditions. It doesn't matter *how* you came to diverge, it's the fact that you *do* diverge. When it comes

2   Judy Singer, *Neurodiversity: The Birth of an Idea* (Lexington, KY: Judy Singer, 2017).

to functioning differently, this can refer to thinking, processing, interpreting, feeling, communicating, socializing, behaving and more.

Asasumasu is responsible for the creation of the term 'neurodivergent' and started using it in 2000 throughout their advocacy work and social media.[3] Kassiane has repeatedly stated that neurodivergent is a tool of inclusion, not exclusion.

Neuronormativity
Neuronormativity refers to a set of standards, expectations and norms that centre a particular way of functioning, thinking, feeling, behaving, learning, communicating and more as the right way to function.

Neurotypical
Neurotypical is a term to describe an individual whose functioning falls within dominant neuronormative standards and norms that centre a particular way of thinking, feeling, communicating, behaving and more. Neurotypical is the opposite of neurodivergent (someone who diverges), and it is not a negative word but a neutral word. 'Neurotypical' dates back to the early 1990s on early Autistic listserv conversations that predate any usage on a website.

Neurodiversity Movement
The Neurodiversity Movement is a social justice movement that seeks rights, equality and inclusion for neurodivergent individuals as well as seeking the end of the marginalization of neurodivergent individuals.

---

3   Kassiane Asasumasu, 'PSA from the Actual Coiner of Neurodivergent', Tumblr, 12 June 2015. www.tumblr.com/sherlocksflataffect/121295972384/psa-from-the-actual-coiner-of-neurodivergent

Neurodiversity Paradigm

The Neurodiversity Paradigm is a specific framework based on the concept of neurodiversity being a natural form of diversity and the idea of a normal or healthy brain as a social construct. It is a new way of viewing, understanding and supporting neurodivergent individuals where we don't default to pathologizing people whose functioning diverges from dominant neuronormative standards.

Pathologization/pathologizing

The practice/act of characterizing a behaviour, emotion, thought or trait as abnormal or an indicator of an illness, disease or disorder.

Proprioception

Proprioception is one our less known senses that is responsible for our awareness of our body including where it is (position) and what it is doing (movement).

Privilege

Privilege refers to the unearned social power, rights and advantages awarded to individuals by society because they are a part of a dominant social identity or group. Privilege can operate on a personal, cultural and institutional or system level.

Pathology Paradigm

The Pathology Paradigm is the dominant framework or lens in which we currently view neurodivergent individuals. It is based on the assumption that any deviance or divergence from what is 'normal' is actually a deficit, disorder or pathology and sorts people into boxes of right or wrong, normal or abnormal.

Social model of disability

The social model of disability believes that disability doesn't necessarily result from our differences but from the barriers and exclusion that occur within society and our environments. Under the social model of disability, disabled people are whole, unbroken people who deserve accommodations and adjustments within society where they can participate fully.

The medical model	The social model
The individual is disabled by their abnormalities or deficits.	The individual is disabled based on differences and barriers in attitudes, environment, society, etc.
Individuals are seen as broken, abnormal damaged or disordered versions of people.	Disabled individuals are a part of the valid diversity of human beings.
Individuals need to be fixed, cured, treated or prevented.	Individuals have a right to autonomy and choice when it comes to their own lives.

Special interests

Special interests are interests or hobbies that are meaningful to Autistic individuals and bring many benefits from comfort, joy, knowledge, skill building and community.

Stimming

Stimming is a functional behaviour that has a role in self-soothing, regulation, expressing emotions, communication and more. Everyone stims one way or another, but some individuals such as Autistic people and ADHDers need to stim more!

Sensory processing

Sensory processing refers to the way individuals perceive, organize and interpret information through their senses including sight, sound, taste, smell, touch, proprioception, interoception and vestibular.

Sensory overload

Sensory overload is the overstimulation of one or more of your body's senses due to sensory input. Sensory overload is common when an individual has a higher sensitivity to certain sensory input.

Stigma

Stigma refers to negative attitudes, stereotypes, beliefs and associations that both society and individuals hold against people due to their particular characteristics or identities.

System

System is a term to describe a group who have multiple selves within one body.

Unmasking

Unmasking is the act or process of meeting your neurodivergent needs and honouring your traits and behaviours by not hiding or suppressing them.

White supremacy

'White supremacy is a racist ideology that is based upon the belief that white people are superior in many ways to people of other races and that therefore, white people should be dominant over other races. White supremacy is not just an attitude or a way of thinking. It also extends to how systems and institutions are structured to uphold this white dominance.'[4]

---

4   Layla F. Saad, *Me and White Supremacy* (Naperville, IL: Sourcebooks, 2020).

CHAPTER 3

The Neurodiversity Movement

When something is a movement, it means there is a change or development that a group of individuals are working towards where there is a common goal, whether it's fighting for equality or ending injustice. While there can often be different ways of achieving the common goal within a movement, it's still about achieving the same outcome, so a movement can be made up of various individuals, groups and communities who all have the same goal.

I want to talk about the Neurodiversity Movement, but before I do, I want to take you on a little history lesson through some other important movements. I believe that without learning about these other crucial movements, our understanding of the Neurodiversity Movement would be incomplete. I also believe it's important to understand these other movements because the Neurodiversity Movement is also for everyone within these movements.

Consumer Movement

The Consumer Movement, also known as the Survivor Movement in some circles, is similar to movements by other communities who have experienced systemic oppression and marginalization. The Consumer Movement took off in the late 1960s alongside other important civil rights movements such as the Women's Movement, which fought for equality and against discrimination, and the Gay Rights Movement. In fact, we can actually trace its history back to the late nineteenth and early twentieth centuries where survivors and patients wrote about their psychiatric experiences. While the Consumer/Survivor Movement is a global movement courtesy of many communities, there are a few key players who are considered pioneers or leaders of the movement, including Judi Chamberlin and her 1978 text *On Our Own: Patient-Controlled Alternatives to the Mental Health System*[1] and a number of other groups that began in the 1970s due to this movement, including the Insane Liberation Front, founded in 1970 in Portland, Oregon, the Mental Patients Liberation Project, founded in 1971 in both New York City and Boston, and the Network Against Psychiatric Assault, founded in 1972 in San Francisco.

The Consumer Movement is, above all, a human rights movement dedicated to fighting for the rights and treatment of consumers and survivors of the psychiatric system, and it became a pressing issue because consumers were being forcibly institutionalized, forcibly medicated, and often subjected to extreme harm and abuse. The Consumer Movement argues for madness not to be seen as an illness or disorder but as an alternative state or way of being. Instead of focusing on healing, fixing and recovering, they believed the goal was accepting their unique differences and fighting for society to change to accept these differences rather than punish and fix these differences. The Consumer/Survivor Movement continues to grow today, and you can find their efforts most

---

1   Judi Chamberlin, *On Our Own: Patient-Controlled Alternatives to the Mental Health System* (Portland, OR: Hawthorn Books, 1978).

strongly represented in advocacy, peer support and policy change at a systemic level.

Mad Pride

Mad Pride was founded by four people with lived experience of mental health conditions and navigating the mental health system: Mark Roberts, Robert Dellar, Pete Shaughnessy and Simon Barnett.[2] The Consumer Movement was underway, which was all about the rights of mental health service users, but they wanted something more – something that resembled a celebration of their madness, especially when stigma was rampant in the media. Mad Pride argues for an identity of madness rather than an identity of shame and stigma. It is a political movement against the stigma and violence faced by people living with mental illnesses and psychiatric disabilities, where we have reclaimed the term 'mad' and deprived it of its negative connotations. Instead, we are proudly mad because to be mad isn't to be bad at all. When we think of mental illness, we tend to think of behaviours, states and experiences that are bad or associated with suffering or negative consequences. Mad Pride, however, rejects the idea that all experiences associated with mental illness lead to suffering and instead offers an alternative explanation: that these behaviours, states of being and experiences challenge social norms and values. Our various states of madness – such as seeing visions and hearing voices, altered emotional states and more – aren't actually inherently negative but are dependent on our understanding as well as the level of support and accommodations we are given in society.

While Mad Pride still recognizes that there is distress, challenges

---

2   Amelia Abraham, 'Remembering Mad Pride, the movement that celebrated mental illness', VICE, 18 November 2016. www.vice.com/en/article/7bxqxa/mad-pride-remembering-the-uks-mental-health-pride-movement

and difficulties associated with these experiences, this movement asks us to consider whether experiencing distress and difficulties requires us to label our experiences as an illness or disorder. Perhaps it depends on how the person interprets the experiences, and that's what Mad Pride is there for – to provide an alternative framework for interpreting one's experiences. Most importantly, Mad Pride calls for society to challenge what we consider to be good or bad, normal or abnormal and right or wrong when it comes to human experiences. On a similar note, we also have to consider who actually has the right to determine when someone's experiences become bad or abnormal. I would like you to remember this because it is something that the Neurodiversity Paradigm also adopts and argues strongly for, too.

Disability Justice

Disability Justice is a movement that was built and developed by Black, Indigenous and people of colour. It was first imagined in 2005 by Sins Invalid co-founder Patty Berne and Mia Mingus and eventually, Stacy Milbern, Leroy Moore, Eli Clare and Sebastian Margaret.[3] Why? Well, they noticed that a lot of the disability conversation was actually centring the white, heteronormative, cisgender experience. In a way, they created a second wave of the Disability Rights Movement known as Disability Justice.

> Disability Justice challenges the idea that our worth as individuals has to do with our ability to perform as productive members of society. It insists that our worth is inherent and tied to the liberation of all beings.[4]

3   Patty Berne and Sins Invalid, *Skin, Tooth, and Bone: The Basis of Movement Is Our People: A Disability Justice Primer* (Berkeley, CA: Sins Invalid, 2019).
4   Nomy Lamm, 'This is Disability Justice', The Body Is Not an Apology, 2 September 2015. https://thebodyisnotanapology.com/magazine/this-is-disability-justice

Disability Justice was created because the Disability Rights Movement wasn't enough for the dismantling of systems. While the Disability Rights Movement established civil rights for disabled people, it lacked an understanding of intersectionality and didn't address the root cause of this discrimination. There is no one who can say it better than the founder of the Disability Justice Movement and Sins Invalid co-founder Patty Berne:

> While a concrete and radical move forward toward justice for disabled people, the Disability Rights Movement simultaneously invisiblized the lives of peoples who live at intersecting junctures of oppression – disabled people of color, immigrants with disabilities, queers with disabilities, trans and gender non-conforming people with disabilities, people with disabilities who are houseless, people with disabilities who are incarcerated, people with disabilities who have had their ancestral lands stolen, amongst others.[5]

Disability Justice recognized that it had to be so much more than just advocating for rights; it had to be about dismantling the very systems in which disabled people were treated and seen as less than.

Sins Invalid have done wonderful work already by creating a Disability Justice Framework and identifying the ten principles of Disability Justice[6] which will hopefully provide an understanding of this movement:

5   Sins Invalid, *Skin, Tooth, and Bone: A Disability Justice Primer* (Sins Invalid, 2016). Accessed 28 October 2022 at www.sinsinvalid.org/disability-justice-primer
6   Patricia Berne, Aurora Levins Morales, David Langstaff and Sins Invalid, 'Ten principles of disability justice', *WSQ: Women's Studies Quarterly* 46, nos 1-2 (2018): 227-230. https://doi.org/10.1353/wsq.2018.0003

TEN PRINCIPLES OF DISABILITY JUSTICE

Principle	What does it mean?
Intersection-ality	We must recognize how ableism intersects with racism, trans-phobia, sexism and white supremacy, which are all supported by capitalism and how the experience of disability is shaped by race, gender, class and gender expression.
Leadership of those most impacted	In order to truly have liberation from oppression, individuals with lived experience who know the most about systems of oppression must lead the movement.
Anti-capitalist politic	It is anti-capitalist because our bodies and minds do not conform to capitalism's concept of normal and productivity. Human worth or value is not defined by what or how much someone can produce.
Cross-movement solidarity	Disability Justice provides a new framework for other social justice movements to understand disability and ableism, and to provide a united front.
Recognizing wholeness	It recognizes that disabled individuals are whole people regardless of their ability to meet capitalist society's idea of productivity or functioning.
Sustainability	Disability Justice recognizes that we must respect our needs and energy and pace ourselves when working towards justice and liberation.
Commitment to cross-disability solidarity	It recognizes and values all insights, participation and lived experience of all individuals, including individuals with physi-cal disabilities, individuals who identify as chronically ill, mad, psychiatric survivor or neurodivergent.
Interdepend-ence	It recognizes independence, and which colonization and white supremacy values shouldn't be the goal; instead, inter-dependence should be seen as valid. Disability Justice works towards meeting each other's needs without relying on state solutions that reinforce control over our lives.
Collective access	Disability Justice explores and creates new ways of doing things that go beyond normativity as well as recognizing that all access needs are valid because everyone has various capacities in various environments.
Collective liberation	In Disability Justice, no mind or body can be left behind in the fight for liberation and justice.

Hearing Voices Movement

The Hearing Voices Movement is a grassroots movement between mental health professionals and people with lived experience of voice hearing that began in the 1980s in the Netherlands. It can be traced back to Patsy Hague, a Dutch voice hearer, as well as Marius Romme, a psychiatrist, and Sandra Escher, who both led further research into exploring alternative understandings of voice hearing in order to challenge the traditional pathology model.[7]

One of the most important messages of the Hearing Voices Movement is that hearing voices is a common and normal variation of human experience rather than a disorder or an unwell brain. The Hearing Voices Movement is responsible for developing a new framework for understanding voices and visions in the context of a person's culture, history, relationships, socioeconomic status, stressors, trauma and more. It is based on the assumption that experiences like hearing voices or seeing visions are just one part of the spectrum of human responses to our environment and that we shouldn't view these experiences as a disease, disorder or problem. Instead, the movement recognizes these experiences as an understandable human experience. It isn't necessarily hearing the voices that is the problem; it's the difficulties in coping with hearing voices and the relationship and meaning people may have with their voices that pose difficulties. It is through this new understanding that the Hearing Voices Movement aims to end the isolation, discrimination, abuse and coercive treatments of voice hearers.

I think it's important to mention that the Hearing Voices Movement doesn't deny that recovery is possible but instead argues

---

7   Rory Neirin Higgs, 'Reconceptualizing psychosis: The Hearing Voices Movement and social approaches to health', *Health and Human Rights Journal* 22, no. 1 (June 2020): 133–144. www.hhrjournal.org/2020/06/reconceptualizing-psychosis-the-hearing-voices-movement-and-social-approaches-to-health

for a new definition of recovery where recovery doesn't have to involve getting rid of the voices but learning to cope and live with them through acceptance and building meaning and coping with voice hearing. The Hearing Voices Network in the UK says this about recovery:

> At the Hearing Voices Network, we use the word recovery to mean 'living the life you choose, not the life others choose for you' (whether those others are family, friends, workers or voices). Many people who hear voices simply don't need to recover - they are already living lives that they love. The voices might enhance their wellbeing, or their experiences may simply not detract from it.[8]

Autism Rights Movement

The Autism Rights Movement, also known as the Autistic Self-Advocacy Movement, is a social justice and civil rights movement started by Autistic adults with the primary demand to not see Autism as a disorder but as a different way of being. You can trace the Autistic Rights Movement to the 1990s when the internet came about and provided more text-based communication for Autistic individuals to connect with each other. It was through mailing lists and servers where the Autistic community was congregating that the beginning of what we know as the Autism Rights Movement came about. While I don't have the word count to name every individual, group or organization responsible for the rise of the Autism Rights Movement, I can surely name some notable ones. When it comes to organizations, Autism Network International (ANI) deserves a significant mention as I'm pretty sure they were probably the first

---

8   National Hearing Voices Network. Accessed 17 October 2022 at www.hearing-voices.org

Autistic-led Autism organization in a world of neurotypical-led Autism organizations. Autism Network International was founded in 1992 by a small group of Autistic people who had connected through a pen-pal programme, and it was through attending Autism conferences run by and for neurotypical parents and realizing they could create their own Autistic-led organization instead of relying on neurotypical-led organizations that the ANI was founded. In fact, it was ANI and their community of Autistic individuals who came up with the term 'neurotypical', as they wanted to move away from referring to non-Autistic people and people without neurological conditions as 'normal'. If you would like to learn about the full history of ANI and how it came to be, you should check out Jim Sinclair's article, 'Autism Network International: The development of a community and its culture'.[9]

While Aspies For Freedom (AFF) was founded much later, in 2004, this group was also at the forefront of the Autism Rights Movement where their aim was to educate the public that Autism came with more strengths than weaknesses, which was the dominant narrative at the time. AFF regularly campaigned against the idea of a cure. AFF is also responsible for creating Autistic Pride Day and while Asperger's is an outdated and harmful term, which I do not promote or endorse, we cannot deny the Aspies For Freedom group as a prominent part of the Autism Rights Movement.

There are also a number of notable individuals who are responsible for the development of the Autism Rights Movement including Amanda Baggs who wrote for Autistics.org, a popular anti-cure website; Michelle Dawson who challenged the ethics of applied behavioural analysis; Joe Mele who held anti-cure protests; Jim Sinclair who co-founded ANI and wrote one of the best-known anti-cure essays, 'Don't Mourn for Us'; and Donna Williams, another co-founder of ANI and Autistic author. I would say Jim Sinclair was one of the very first individuals to put forward an anti-cure stance and probably built part of the foundation of the Autism Rights Movement.

The Autism Rights Movement had multiple purposes that boiled down to advocating for Autistic individuals to have the same rights, opportunities and quality of life as anyone else. The goals of the Autism Rights Movement included getting rid of applied behavioural analysis (ABA), removing other inhumane treatments and challenging the language and descriptions of Autism. When so much of the narrative was around Autism being a tragedy that must be eradicated and cured, the Autism Rights Movement was advocating for the opposite – and, honestly, we're still fighting this narrative to this day. Autistic individuals are against curing Autism because we believe that if you remove the Autism, you would get a completely different person because Autism is such a fundamental part of us and who we are. I think Jim Sinclair explained it best in his anti-cure essay, 'Don't Mourn for Us':

> It is not possible to separate autism from the person. Therefore, when parents say, 'I wish my child did not have autism', what they're really saying is, 'I wish the autistic child I have did not exist and I had a different (non-autistic) child instead.' Read that again. This is what we hear when you mourn over our existence. This is what we hear when you pray for a cure. This is what we know, when you tell us of your fondest hopes and dreams for us: that your greatest wish is that one day we will cease to be, and strangers you can love will move in behind our faces.[10]

10 Sarah Pripas-Kapit, 'Historicizing Jim Sinclair's "Don't Mourn for Us": A Cultural and Intellectual History of Neurodiversity's First Manifesto', in *Autistic Community and the Neurodiversity Movement*, ed. Steven K. Kapp (Singapore: Palgrave Macmillan, 2020), 23–39. https://doi.org/10.1007/978-981-13-8437-0_2

The Neurodiversity Movement

The Neurodiversity Movement is a social justice and civil rights movement, and it's important to understand that even though the Neurodiversity Movement was born from the Autism Rights Movement, the Neurodiversity Movement is a separate movement with its own goals and principles that argues for equality, respect and full inclusion for all neurodivergent individuals. I think it's also essential that we recognize that the Neurodiversity Movement has also grown from the Disability Rights Movement, while the Disability Rights Movement was born from the Civil Rights Movement which fought for equality and freedom for Black people and other people of colour. In saying that, we need to acknowledge and appreciate the advocacy and work of Black activists and advocates.

I think it's also important to know that it is a leaderless social movement. The Neurodiversity Movement isn't run by any one individual, group or organization, but obviously, there are a number of wonderful individuals who have contributed to the development of the movement. Two of the most notable individuals are Judy Singer, who introduced the term 'neurodiversity' into academia and Harvey Blume, who popularized the term in a 1998 issue of *The Atlantic*. Judy Singer writes on her blog that in her original conception of the term, 'neurodiversity' was meant to be 'an umbrella term as a possible name for a civil rights movement for the neurological minorities beginning to coalesce around the pioneering work of the Autistic Self-Advocacy Movement'.[11]

Basically, Judy Singer recognized that there were other groups of individuals alongside Autistic individuals who were also devalued, misunderstood and discriminated against and who didn't fit

---

[11]   Judy Singer, 'Neurodiversity: Definition and discussion', Reflections on Neurodiversity. Accessed 10 September 2022 at https://neurodiversity2.blogspot.com/p/what.html

into the Autism Rights Movement but were also worthy of being seen as valid humans with access to the same rights and equality, free from discrimination and unfair treatment. I think it's important to note that the Neurodiversity Movement is often led by certain neurodivergent individuals, namely Autistic and ADHD individuals as well as individuals with learning differences. As the movement is predominantly led by these individuals, it means society tends to view the movement as a movement only for these individuals, which actually doesn't align with the intentions and purposes of this movement. The Neurodiversity Movement is still in its growing phase, and I genuinely hope we can make room for all neurodivergent individuals to identify with the movement.

While there isn't any set definition of the Neurodiversity Movement, Judy Singer says there are four common goals or purposes of this particular movement which I have paraphrased below:[12]

- shifting mainstream perceptions of marginalized neurodivergent individuals

- replacing negative, deficit-based stereotypes of neurodivergent individuals with a more balanced narrative of their strengths and needs

- finding valued roles for neurodivergent individuals

- acknowledging that society benefits from the inclusion of neurodivergent individuals.

12 'What Is Neurodiversity?', Reflections on the Neurodiversity Paradigm, accessed 28 October 2022. https://neurodiversity2.blogspot.com/p/what.html

I would also like to add a few more goals of the Neurodiversity Movement:

- ending the neglect, abuse and punishment of neurodivergent individuals as well as coercive treatment that ignores the autonomy of neurodivergent individuals

- fighting for accessibility and accommodations within society for neurodivergent individuals

- providing equal living, education, employment and housing opportunities for neurodivergent individuals.

I also want to point out that there are some similarities in regard to the messages and goals between the Neurodiversity Movement and other movements. Just as the Deaf Rights Movement advocates against the supremacy of spoken communication, the Neurodiversity Movement advocates for society to see all types of communication as valid where neurodivergent individuals deserve accommodations to make communication more accessible. While Disability Justice says all bodies are unique and essential, neurodiversity says all minds are unique and essential. Just as Disability Justice says all bodies have strengths as well as needs that have to be met, neurodiversity says all minds have strengths as well as needs that deserve to be met. While the Hearing Voices Movement argues that hearing voices isn't a pathology or a sign of a disease but, instead, just another part of human experience and human diversity, where supporting voice hearers should be about minimizing distress rather than correcting their experiences, the Neurodiversity Movement advocates for neurodivergent individuals to be in charge of the care and support we choose to receive. The Neurodiversity Movement recognizes neurodivergent as an identity similar to the way in which the Deaf Pride Movement recognizes that, for many individuals, being Deaf is a culture and identity rather than a pathology or disease. In fact, many Deaf people feel as though they are actually a cultural and linguistic minority with their own culture, values and language. As Michelle Jay shares, 'a common quote in Deaf culture is: Deaf people can do everything hearing people can do, except hear'.[13] In a way, it makes me think of neurodivergent individuals and how we can do almost everything neurotypical people can do; we just do it differently and often require accommodations and alternative ways of doing things.

As we know, the Neurodiversity Movement is a new movement, which means it's still developing, growing and even adjusting. We've got strides to go when it comes to progress and change, as well as liberation and rights for all neurodivergent individuals. Since we've still got a way to go, I feel that we could take a page or two from the Disability Justice Movement. More specifically, we need to recognize the importance of the principles of Disability Justice as well as how we can apply them to the Neurodiversity Movement. In fact, I believe the Neurodiversity Movement probably needs its own set of principles, so following Sins Invalid's Principles of Disability Justice, I would like to propose these principles:

Leadership by the neurodivergent individuals most impacted

- The Neurodiversity Movement must be led by neurodivergent individuals but, most importantly, it must be led by neurodivergent individuals who hold multiple identities and who know the most about the systems of oppression.

---

13 Michelle Jay, 'Deaf culture values: Deafness', Start ASL, 15 February 2921. www.startasl.com/wp-content/uploads/StartASLlogoFinal-1.png

- We must elevate the voices and work of neurodivergent individuals who are non-speaking, physically disabled, Black, Indigenous, First Nations and people of colour, as well as neurodivergent individuals who are trans, non-binary or otherwise gender diverse.

Intersectionality

- We must consider that every neurodivergent individual has multiple identities where we are not only neurodivergent but also coming from different experiences, including disability, race, gender, sexuality, culture and class.

- We must also consider that, despite being neurodivergent, we all have identities where we may experience privilege as well as oppression.

Anti-capitalist

- The Neurodiversity Movement needs to be anti-capitalist and needs to actively challenge capitalism, especially as neurodivergent individuals' very existence challenges capitalist values and standards.

- The Neurodiversity Movement must recognize that neurodivergent individuals are whole individuals regardless of their ability to meet capitalist society's idea of productivity or functioning.

Honouring the movements that came before

- The Neurodiversity Movement can only reach its potential by recognizing other social justice movements and aligning itself with prison abolition, queer and trans liberation, anti-racism, fat liberation and anti-psychiatry.

- The Neurodiversity Movement must also value and prioritize the lived experience of all individuals including neurodivergent individuals, people of colour, disabled individuals, LGBTQIA+ individuals, as well as individuals who identify as chronically ill, mad or a psychiatric survivor.

Access needs are a right

- The Neurodiversity Movement must advocate for new ways of doing things that challenge neuronormative and capitalist expectations and norms.

- The Neurodiversity Movement recognizes that neurodivergent individuals have needs and challenges requiring support and accommodations that may challenge or be different from Western societal norms and capitalist expectations. However, this doesn't make a person any less whole, worthy or valuable, because access needs are human needs, and every individual has different capacities in various environments and contexts.

- The Neurodiversity Movement must also challenge the concept of independence and move towards recognizing interdependence where all neurodivergent individuals deserve to have their needs met and deserve ways of meeting these needs without relying on systems.

- The Neurodiversity Movement must be accessible for all neurodivergent individuals where there is room for all neurodivergent individuals to participate.

Autonomy for all

- The Neurodiversity Movement must acknowledge that all neurodivergent individuals deserve autonomy in how they choose to live their lives as well as autonomy in deciding what recovery, well-being or functioning means to them.

- The Neurodiversity Movement fights for systems and society to respect the autonomy of neurodivergent individuals.

I believe the Neurodiversity Movement has so much potential because it's still so new; it's kind of like a toddler who hasn't reached all of its milestones yet. It's actually quite exciting and hopeful because there are so many more milestones still to come; it's only up from here for neurodivergent individuals. I truly believe that, which is why I also believe that, in order to get there, we do need some common principles. I believe these are the necessary principles for the Neurodiversity Movement. While the principles I've suggested above aren't perfect or complete, they do constitute a start. Perhaps these principles can be a foundation for individuals and groups to build on. I welcome and call upon individuals, groups and communities to expand upon these principles with their own unique perspectives and lived experience.

I would like to end this chapter with the reminder that, like every other movement, the Neurodiversity Movement is about appreciating the diversity within our society and valuing and respecting differences instead of othering and discriminating against differences.

CHAPTER 4

The Pathology Paradigm

Moving away from disorder

I have to admit that I didn't actually plan for this particular chapter. As I wrote the rest of the book, I started to realize that there was a need for this chapter; that any discussion around the Neurodiversity Paradigm, neurodivergence and neuronormativity would be incomplete if we don't understand why we are fighting and advocating for this paradigm shift, for this movement. I don't believe we can understand the importance or significance of the term 'neurodivergence' if we do not understand the history, development or implication of the term 'disorder' and the contentious history behind the DSM. I also do not believe we can shift to an alternative framework, the Neurodiversity Paradigm, without recognizing and understanding the dominant framework, the Pathology Paradigm, and how it has and continues to harm and oppress so many individuals.

I also want to pay homage to the individual who is responsible for the naming and defining of the Pathology Paradigm and that is Dr Nick Walker, an Autistic author. I was introduced to the Pathology Paradigm through a chapter in her book *Neuroqueer Heresies*, entitled 'Throw Away the Master's Tools: Liberating Ourselves from the Pathology Paradigm',[1] and while this chapter focuses on moving away from the Pathology Paradigm to a Neurodiversity Paradigm in the context of Autism, I couldn't help but wonder what moving away from a Pathology Paradigm to a Neurodiversity Paradigm could mean for every neurodivergent individual.

Understanding the Pathology Paradigm

I would like to start by sharing what a paradigm actually is. A paradigm is simply a name for a set of principles, ideas or assumptions that provides a framework for how we view, interpret or understand something. When we talk about a paradigm shift, we're talking about changing how we view or understand something. As Dr Nick Walker says, 'a paradigm is the lens through which we view reality',[2] and in the case of the Pathology Paradigm, it is a framework or lens through which we view and understand individuals and their differences, responses, behaviours and functioning. It is the framework in which psychiatry, psychology and the medical model operates. It is the lens through which psychiatry and psychology understand us – and the truth is, they aren't understanding us at all. You could say their lens is clouded with harmful assumptions and biases. In fact, their lens is rooted in the concept of normality, and any deviance from this socially constructed normality is unwell or sick. Put simply, this lens has the wrong prescription that's causing more harm than good.

---

1   Nick Walker, 'Throw Away the Master's Tools: Liberating Ourselves from the Pathology Paradigm', in *Neuroqueer Heresies: Notes on the Neurodiversity Paradigm, Autistic Empowerment, and Postnormal Possibilities* (Fort Worth, TX: Autonomous Press, 2021).
2   Nick Walker, *Neuroqueer Heresies: Notes on the Neurodiversity Paradigm, Autistic Empowerment, and Postnormal Possibilities* (Fort Worth, TX: Autonomous Press, 2021).

Let's talk about this lens. As you now know, a paradigm is a set of principles or assumptions and, like every paradigm, the Pathology Paradigm has a set of assumptions on which the entire framework is based. Just like most assumptions, these assumptions aren't necessarily correct, but the Pathology Paradigm has been our dominant framework or model for so long that they've become a given. Dr Nick Walker has defined the following assumptions underpinning the Pathology Paradigm:[3]

- There is one right or normal way for brains or minds to function.

- If your functioning falls outside of this one right or normal way, there is something wrong with you and you are labelled with a disorder, a disease.

- If your functioning and your ways of thinking, behaving, feeling, processing, communicating and more diverge from the supposed right way, then they must be fixed.

Basically, the Pathology Paradigm is based on the assumption that any deviance or divergence from the dominant standard of normal is actually a deficit, disorder or pathology – an illness or disease residing within the individual. It achieves this through the *Diagnostic and Statistical Manual of Mental Disorders* (the DSM) by sorting people into boxes of right or wrong, normal or abnormal and ordered or disordered, which results in us believing there is something wrong with us for simply existing the way we do.

At the root of these assumptions is the biomedical model that

---

3 Nick Walker, *Neuroqueer Heresies: Notes on the Neurodiversity Paradigm, Autistic Empowerment, and Postnormal Possibilities* (Fort Worth, TX: Autonomous Press, 2021).

argues any deviation, any divergence, is a result of brain diseases and biological abnormalities that must be cured and treated. In a way, it makes sense that we automatically argue that mental disorders are brain diseases that can be treated with drugs to cure and fix because it automatically provides a solution that we are so eagerly searching for. We tend to appreciate the easiest and simplest explanation even if it may be incorrect. We appreciate a quick fix, which is what viewing things as a disease that we can get rid of gives us. While the Pathology Paradigm may use the biomedical model as a scientific argument for its existence, it should be seen for what it actually is: a social construct rooted in cultural and social norms. That's not to say that individuals cannot find medication helpful, but when it comes to the Pathology Paradigm, medication is often the default approach based on the assumption that individuals need to be fixed, treated or cured.

Understanding the term 'disorder'
If neurodivergent aligns with the Neurodiversity Paradigm, disorder aligns with the Pathology Paradigm. The origin and basis of the word 'disorder' has always had negative connotations – it was created to describe someone who is unwell, faulty, wrong or broken. You might think that disorder is a medical term that signifies a disease or illness, but really it is a social term based on one's adherence to dominant social and cultural norms. In fact, our understanding of what is a disorder is based on the idea that there is one right way for people to feel, think, learn, communicate, behave and function. Basically, disorder is a social construct based on normality, and as neurodiversity demonstrates, normal is a social construct. When we consider all of this, we need to ask ourselves: Is the concept of a disorder actually valid?

Let's do a little thought exercise. If someone asked you to describe the traits of someone who is 'normal', would you actually be able to? If you feel like it, grab a pen and paper, your laptop or whatever device suits your needs and come up with a list of traits that you believe meet the criteria for being labelled as a 'normal' person. As you examine this list, ask yourself if these are truly traits of a 'normal' person or if these are actually a set of expectations, standards and norms.

Within the current version of the DSM, DSM-5,[4] a mental disorder is defined as a disturbance that reflects a dysfunction in someone's processes and functioning that is usually associated with distress in social, occupational and other activities. In order to reflect a dysfunction in psychological, biological or developmental processes, there has to be an agreed-upon idea of which psychological, biological or developmental processes are normal, healthy or functional. If we recognize neurodiversity, we have to remember that there's actually no such thing as one healthy brain. We need to ask ourselves: What is dysfunctional?

As I've discussed above, there's actually no real definition of normal; normal doesn't exist because it is a social construct. There is also a caveat within the definition of a mental disorder, too; an expectable or culturally approved response isn't a mental disorder. However, this means that if expectable responses or culturally approved responses are not a disorder, any responses that are not expectable or culturally approved are disorders. We must ask ourselves: Who defines what is expected and who defines what is a culturally appropriate response? At the end of the day, the DSM and the construction of disorders were built on the loudest voices in the room at the time. Most importantly, the constructions of disorders are rooted in racism, colonialism, sexism, transphobia, homophobia and ableism. In order to understand this, it might be helpful to understand the history and development of the DSM.

4   *Diagnostic and Statistical Manual of Mental Disorders Fifth Edition: DSM-5* (Arlington, VA: American Psychiatric Association, 2017).

The DSM

The DSM is the primary arbiter of what is disordered and non-disordered. I guess you could call it a product of the Pathology Paradigm or even a tool within the Pathology Paradigm. If there is one thing to know about the DSM, it is that it has always been more political than scientific. In fact, the inclusion of what is or isn't a disorder is often made by a vote rather than any actual scientific data. Dr Thomas Insel, who has rejected the DSM, has stated that 'the weakness is its lack of validity. Unlike our definitions of ischaemic heart disease, lymphoma, or AIDS, the DSM diagnoses are based on a consensus about clusters of clinical symptoms, not any objective laboratory measure.'[5]

While the DSM provides a common language to understand collective experiences, it also serves a multitude of other purposes, from deciding who receives disability payments to deciding who is eligible for insurance and who receives accommodations and support. Put simply, without the DSM, therapists don't get paid and individuals can't access therapy. The DSM also plays a part in legal decisions, from child custody disputes to assigning punishments. Most significantly, it shapes the direction of research as well as the development and approval of new drugs. The DSM also forms the basis of learning for a number of professions including (but probably not limited to) psychiatrists, psychologists, social workers, nurses, therapists and counsellors. In a way, the DSM has made itself indispensable to society and the systems within it.

I would be remiss if I didn't state that the field of psychiatry and psychology as well as the DSM, for all intents and purposes, is a colonial system built upon white supremacy. The entire foundation of psychiatry and psychology was pretty much shaped by white colonizers in the late 18th and 19th centuries, which is evident when you consider the history.

The history of the DSM

The first edition of the DSM as we know it appeared in 1952, and the manual was just a thin, spiral-bound booklet with only 32 pages to define 106 diagnoses. In the 1980s, the third edition of the DSM listed 265 diagnoses, and now we are up to the fifth edition, known as the DSM-5,[6] which is a giant book of 947 pages with 300 diagnoses. Did you know that the development of the DSM dates back all the way to the early 18th century? Its initial goal was to collect statistical information on the frequency of insanity. In the 1840 census, the government collected data on insanity, and by 1880, there were a number of categories within this statistical manual that were distinguished as: mania, melancholia, monomania, paresis, dementia, dipsomania and epilepsy. Obviously, this was just a manual on statistics, so after the Second World War, military psychiatrists found this manual was a bit useless when it came to soldiers, individuals and their wartime and post-wartime experiences. In response, the first edition of the DSM was developed in order to reflect the experiences of soldiers and individuals. In 1952, The American Psychiatric Association published the first edition of the *Diagnostic and Statistical Manual of Mental Disorders* based on the World Health Organization's International Classification of Diseases known as the ICD-6 and, surprisingly, the military system.[7]

However, in the 1960s and 1970s, the DSM began to recive a

---

6   *Diagnostic and Statistical Manual of Mental Disorders Fifth Edition: DSM-5* (Arlington, VA: American Psychiatric Association, 2017).
7   Allan V. Horwitz, 'DSM-I and DSM-II', in *The Encyclopedia of Clinical Psychology* (Wiley Online Library, 2014), 1-6. https://doi.org/10.1002/9781118625392.wbecp012

number of criticisms and was even losing its legitimacy.[8] Insurance companies and government officials – rightly so – were also starting to question the validity of mental health disorders due to the lack of specific criteria and measurable outcomes. There's also another significant change in relation to all this – a new rule by the Food and Drug Administration was introduced which meant that psychiatric medication could only be identified as a treatment if it was for a recognizable and specific disorder. I also want to point out another part of the rule that the Food and Drug Administration began to enforce: treatment of any psychiatric drug couldn't be for general distress or any problems arising from an individual's own environment.[9] As expected, this had a significant impact on the use of medications for mental health disorders. This is because pharmaceutical companies needed to prove the effectiveness of drugs, which required evidence from clinical studies. In order for pharmaceutical companies to prove the effectiveness of drugs and for insurance companies to be willing to pay, disorders needed to be defined as an illness that was treatable.

To put it more simply, psychiatry needed to invent specific disorders with distinguishable criteria in order to access medication as a treatment option and retain funding. At this time, the public was gaining more confidence in medicine. In fact, the public's trust and confidence in medicine was highest in the 1970s because of the advances in surgical techniques, drug discovery, immunization and, of course, the control of infectious diseases such as polio.[10] In order for the concept of disorders to maintain its legitimacy, psychiatry

8   Gary Greenberg, 'The Cult of DSM,' *Psychotherapy Networker*, March/April 2014. www.psychotherapynetworker.org/article/cult-dsm

9   Allan V. Horwitz, 'DSM-I and DSM-II', in *The Encyclopedia of Clinical Psychology* (Wiley Online Library, 2014), 1–6. https://doi.org/10.1002/9781118625392.wbecp012

10 Robert J. Blendon and John M. Benson, 'Trust in medicine, the health system & public health', *Daedalus* 151, no. 4 (2022), 67–82. https://doi.org/10.1162/daed_a_01944

needed to demonstrate that mental health disorders were illnesses or diseases – something that medicine could actually treat or cure. This is also where the chemical imbalance myth originated. In order for a mental health disorder to be treatable or curable, there needed to be a biological cause, which is why, in the 1970s, mental health disorders began to be defined as chemical imbalances and problems with neurotransmitters.

We really cannot ignore the role insurance companies and the pharmaceutical industry played in the creation of the DSM...which brings us to 1980 when the third edition of the DSM was published. In this edition, there were a number of differences. Everything was now defined as a disorder instead of a reaction or response – a common feature in the previous edition – and each disorder came with a checklist of criteria. The most significant difference was that there were now 265 disorders, which means there were over 100 new disorders. I just want to reframe this if that's okay with you.

In the 1960s when the second edition was published, there were 126 disorders. In 1980, when the third edition was published, there were 265 disorders. As the team behind the DSM didn't begin working on the third edition until 1974, that means it only took them six years to come up with more than 136 new disorders and create distinguishable criteria for all 265 disorders. While it's easy to assume we've discovered a number of new diseases or illnesses in the form of mental health disorders, I don't believe this is the case. We've merely invented and constructed new labels based on society's concept of normality.

In order to retain legitimacy as well as make money – something we cannot ignore – more than 100 disorders were suddenly found. That seems a bit suspicious to me – and if not suspicious, at least a bit fast. You know the saying 'Don't believe everything you read'? It's rather fitting, but I'm guessing that wasn't a thing back then because, of course, insurance companies ate it up, society ate it up and psychiatry's legitimacy was restored. It really didn't take long for the DSM to become the basis for understanding and categorizing mental illnesses and mental disorders, but it wasn't just clinicians who happily adopted this new concept but researchers, government officials, pharmaceutical companies, the judicial system, educators and teachers, and even insurance companies. I would even go as far as saying that most of Western society adopted this book.

It's important to know that the DSM has been criticized from the very beginning of its inception because there was an utter lack of clarity when it came to differentiating between normal and abnormal responses and behaviours. I'm not the first person to criticize the DSM and I will not be the last. In fact, a number of psychiatrists and psychologists as well as numerous individuals have critiqued the existence of psychiatry and, consequently, how the DSM has always had the primary purpose of maintaining social control and social order.

I'm sure you can probably guess who was (and still is) at the top of the social order: white, straight and cisgendered men – which meant that anyone who wasn't white, straight or a man was controlled, oppressed, tortured and even killed by labelling people as disordered. As Vesper Moore says, 'anyone who does not fit a cis, white, hetero, patriarchal state of being could be deemed "mad" because their identity is against the conventions of what exists in our society'.[11]

In 1851, Dr Samuel Cartwright came up with the term 'drapetomania', which was defined as a mental illness that compelled

---

11 Institute for the Development of the Human Arts (@idha_nyc), 'The mental health system is steeped in oppressive ideologies and histories', Instagram, 12 March 2022. www.instagram.com/p/Ca-DrqLO6f1

enslaved Black people to run away.[12] Basically, it was decided that Black people weren't running away from slavery; they were running away because they were mentally ill. Drapetomania was one of the first mental disorders. It was created by a slaveholder's doctor because they believed Black people were slave-bound so it was unimaginable that they would want to run away. Therefore, a disorder was the only explanation. You might be thinking, 'Oh, but that was so long ago', but it didn't stop there. While slavery was technically abolished, white people still viewed Black people as inferior and in need of eradicating, which brings us to the 1920s when Black women were diagnosed with mental disorders and legally sterilized in order to prevent them from having children. As this practice didn't end till the 1970s, you can imagine how many Black women suffered at the hands of psychiatry. Of course, it didn't end there because psychiatry found another disorder to target Black people with in the form of schizophrenia. Did you know aggressiveness was only added to the criteria of schizophrenia because white people believed Black men were angry, dangerous and aggressive? In fact, as Dr Jennifer Mullan says:

[In] the 50s, primarily discontented housewives were diagnosed [with] schizophrenia. The anti-racist revolts of the 60s prompted the Diagnostic and Statistical Manual of Mental Disorders (DSM) to change its description of schizophrenia from 'primarily depressed moods' to 'hostility, aggression and delusions of persecution'.[13]

I mean, isn't it awfully convenient that the criteria of schizophrenia

12   Christopher D. Willoughby, 'Running away from Drapetomania: Samuel A. Cartwright, medicine, and race in the antebellum south', *Journal of Southern History* 84, no. 3 (2018): 579-614. https://doi.org/10.1353/soh.2018.0164
13   Dr Jennifer Mullan (@decolonizingtherapy), 'Therapy serves capitalism by diagnosing rage', Instagram, 30 November 2019. www.instagram.com/p/B5d7GV1AGJi

changed in order to suit what society was deeming unacceptable? Instead of recognizing the valid responses to oppression, torture, segregation and poverty, Black men were pathologized and labelled with a disorder which meant that psychiatry was able to medicate them or lock them away – all in the name of maintaining social order or, in other words, maintaining white supremacy.

Similarly, females have also been seen as inferior in the eyes of a male-dominated society, which led to the invention of a female-only mental disorder called hysteria in the 18th century. While hysteria has existed for over 4000 years, often associated with witchcraft and sorcery, it wasn't until the 18th century that it was categorized as a female disease. If you need proof that males viewed females as inferior, Sigmund Freud, the well-known founder of psychoanalysis, actually proposed that hysteria was a result of removing male sexual organs from females. Basically, females were so ridden with grief that they were not male that they became hysterical. In fact, at the time, the recommendation was to marry a penis and, ideally, give birth to a penis because that was as close as they could come to being male.[14]

It's important to note that hysteria was a form of social control in order to keep females in line and in their rightful place: under the control of men. Females were expected to act and behave a certain way; they needed to be submissive, compliant, calm and polite, and if they weren't and if they did anything that was deemed unacceptable female behaviour, they were labelled with hysteria. As a result, females went through hysterectomies, frontal lobotomies and electric shock therapy, and were medicated as well as committed to psychiatric hospitals. While hysteria was finally removed as an

---

14 Ada McVean, 'The history of hysteria,' McGill Office for Science and Society, 31 July 2019. www.mcgill.ca/oss/article/history-quackery/history-hysteria

official disorder within the DSM in the 1980s, we are still quick to label females as hysterical, emotional or irrational to this day.[15]

In 1952, the first *Diagnostic and Statistical Manual of Mental Disorders* was published, and homosexuality, attraction between two men, was listed as a personality disturbance. As you have probably already gathered, homosexuality wasn't added to the DSM because it's a disease or disorder; it was added because it was viewed as a form of deviance and challenged social norms as well as gender norms. Put simply, it was viewed as wrong or abnormal in the eyes of society and therefore it was a disorder that had to be treated in order to fix what was broken. While there were many different treatments, including hypnosis, shock treatment, conversion therapy, abstinence and even lobotomy, they obviously didn't a cure a thing. Of course, some psychiatrists did claim they were successful, only to admit later on that no one actually stayed 'cured'. If you were being tortured and brainwashed, you would probably pretend to be cured, too. While homosexuality was removed as a disorder in the 1980s – which we owe to the Gay Rights' lobbying and advocacy – the damage was done. To this day, the impact of the pathologization of gender and sexuality is still going strong, which is evident in the ever-present stigma within society and, more specifically, trans people requiring a medical professional to sign off on gender-affirming procedures.

These are just a few examples of how psychiatry's labelling of people as disordered has been a way to control and oppress certain communities, but we also need to acknowledge what else psychiatry aims to control or, more specifically, uphold and maintain – and that is capitalism. In order to understand how psychiatry upholds capitalism, it's important to recognize that psychiatry and

15 Jessica Taylor, *Sexy but Psycho: How the Patriarchy Uses Women's Trauma Against Them* (London: Constable, 2022).

the development of the DSM evolved right alongside capitalism within society. If you try to trace the beginning of mental illness and mental disorder as a concept, you'll find it coincides with the rise of capitalism. As a result, it was inevitable that capitalism would influence the deciding upon what is or isn't disordered and what is or isn't abnormal behaviour. It's easy to see the impact of capitalism when a significant feature of a disorder is an impairment within workplaces or education. In fact, psychiatry and the DSM reinforce what is, apparently, acceptable behaviour when it comes to work, school, home and within society, but the thing is, most of these acceptable behaviours are whatever benefits capitalism. As capitalism has risen and, along with it, the need for individuals to be productive members of society, so have the criteria for acceptable behaviour when it comes to workplaces. Jesse Meadows, in one of their articles, even counted the number of times that 'work' was mentioned in the DSM and it went from ten mentions in the first DSM to 385 mentions in DSM-5.[16]

A great example when it comes to understanding how capitalism shapes what we consider a disorder is ADHD. As Jesse Meadows, also known as jessethesluggish on Instagram, says, 'The story we are sold about ADHD is not apolitical – it's based on a particular set of values.'[17] If we look at common ADHD traits such as hyperactivity, impulsivity and inattention, these are traits that are often seen as disruptive, abnormal or problematic, but the thing is, these traits weren't actually considered a problem until society introduced mandatory education where children needed to sit compliantly in a small room all day. Bruce Cohen even notes that:

16 Jesse Meadows, 'Would you still have ADHD without capitalism?' Sluggish, 5 July 2022. https://sluggish.substack.com/p/would-you-still-have-adhd-without
17 Jesse Meadows, 'We need critical ADHD studies now', Medium, 5 July 2021. https://jessemeadows.medium.com/we-need-critical-adhd-studies-now-52d4267edd54

the expansion of ADHD from a rare disorder to a popular disease among young people over the past 35 years can be understood as a result of capitalism's need to enforce discipline, compliance, and authority on the future workforce at a younger age.[18]

I mean, I feel as though even our relationship with sleep is another example – us ADHDers are known to have sleep difficulties, but really they're only difficulties because of the pressure to be up at a certain time of day for work or school. If capitalism didn't demand a nine-to-five work schedule, would we still be accused of having sleep difficulties or poor sleep?

Although I go into this further in another chapter, I do need to mention another example of how capitalism shapes what we consider a disorder – this is executive functioning. Executive functioning is a set of skills associated with planning, time management, organization, memory, starting tasks and more, and they're seen as necessary to function in everyday life at work, school and home. Executive dysfunction is when someone has difficulty with these skills, and you'll find that almost every disorder is associated with executive dysfunction from Autism and ADHD to depression and dyslexia to brain injuries. You may be wondering: How does this relate to capitalism? Well, when we experience so-called executive dysfunction, we tend to struggle with things like work, school and getting things done, and capitalism doesn't like that at all. We need to abide by the rules of capitalism, and when we don't, there's a problem. It is much easier to blame the individual than to recognize that the way we expect people to function at work and school just isn't sustainable or realistic. That's exactly how the DSM has been impacted by capitalism; it labels anyone who struggles to meet

18 Bruce M. Z. Cohen, *Psychiatric Hegemony: A Marxist Theory of Mental Illness* (London: Palgrave Macmillan, 2016).

capitalist expectations with a disorder. It's always 'there must be something inherently wrong with the person' and never 'there must be something inherently wrong with the system and its expectations'. Honestly, Jesse Meadows says it perfectly:

> Most people on social media seem to think the set of skills around planning, organizing, focusing, and time management which we call 'executive function' is a structure in the brain, not a concept made up by a bunch of white male doctors who idolize businessmen so much they modeled an entire neurological value system off of them.[19]

Are we actually disordered or are the expectations within our capitalist society unrealistic? As you can tell, there's a lot of negative connotations when it comes to the term 'disorder', and there is a lot of insidious history when it comes to whom psychiatry and the DSM considers disordered, so here are the main points:

- Black people were considered inferior to white people; they were labelled with a disorder.

- Women were viewed as inferior to men; they were labelled with a disorder.

- Gay men and lesbians were viewed as abnormal; they were labelled with a disorder.

- If people struggle to meet capitalistic standards and expectations, they are labelled with a disorder.

19 Jesse Meadows, 'We need critical ADHD studies now', Medium, 5 July 2021. https://jessemeadows.medium.com/we-need-critical-adhd-studies-now-52d4267edd54

- If people function differently, they are labelled with a disorder.

- If people experience distress in response to their environment, they are labelled with a disorder. The problem with this is that it labels valid responses to oppression and trauma as individual defects.

I'm not sure if you've noticed the pattern, but you can see how as soon as someone doesn't fit into certain standards and expectations or an unclear concept of normal, they're viewed as the one with the problem. I say it's an unclear concept of normal because throughout the lifetime of psychiatry and the DSM, there has been this implicit idea of normal but no one ever actually says what normal is. 'Disorder' is a problematic concept, and when we relate it to our personalities, our behaviour, our learning, our emotions, calling someone disordered has always conjured up negative connotations – like bad, wrong, not right, unhealthy, a problem, broken, crazy or in need of fixing. When it comes to the term 'disorder', it implies we are not in the right order, it implies we aren't working properly, it implies our responses are our problem, and it implies our functioning isn't normal. Maybe we are functioning the way we are meant to, maybe our responses are proportionate to the world we exist in, maybe we are in the order we are meant to be, and maybe we are working the way we are meant to work. We truly need to start seeing people as diverse individuals who have the capacity to think, process, learn, feel, behave and exist in infinitely different ways to each other. As Dr Ayesha Khan says:

Mental health systems were built to pathologize people's logical responses, suffering or diverge under systems of oppression. They are a form of victim blaming – where individuals who diverge from or rebel against capitalist/colonial norms are ostracized and diagnosed as mentally ill.[20]

I also want to clarify a couple of things because I don't want anyone to feel as though I'm invalidating or dismissing their challenges or distress. When I challenge the concept of disorder, I am not saying that individuals do not have genuine differences, but I am saying that people are not disordered because of these differences. I am also not saying that people don't experience genuine distress or challenges, but I am saying that we don't have to consider ourselves as broken, abnormal or wrong as 'disorder' implies. It's okay if you feel that disorder is an accurate label for you. I do hope that by reading this book, you can see that an alternative exists, and perhaps you can recognize the implications of using such an oppressive term. If you feel like reflecting on your use of 'disorder' and perhaps trying on a different term, here are some prompts that I've written to help you on this journey:

- What thoughts accompany me when I think of myself as disordered and/or having a disorder?

- How has identifying as disordered impacted how I think and feel about myself?

- How would I think of my difficulties and challenges if I didn't think of myself as disordered?

I wrote this chapter because I wanted to explain why so many of us are fighting to be seen not as someone with a disorder but as

20 Dr Ayesha Kahn (@wokescientist), 'A little note on the main criticisms of mainstream mental health systems under capitalism', Instagram, 28 June 2022. www. instagram.com/p/CfUaW7Huacf

someone who is neurodivergent. I hope by showing the history of psychiatry, the DSM and the inherent pathologizing of humanity that we can see the need for a new framework for understanding our responses, differences, distress and functioning. I reject the default pathologization of human experiences, human responses, distress and functioning. In fact, that is my main criticism of the Pathology Paradigm – that we automatically pathologize different experiences, responses, distress and alternative functioning. I do not believe it allows room for choice or nuance. In fact, it often takes away people's choices. I believe that is what we need to move away from – the inherent and default pathologization of people – and instead move towards allowing people to define their own experiences. Unfortunately, there is no room for people to define their own experiences as this is the only framework on offer. While the Pathology Paradigm that underpins psychiatry and the DSM is the dominant framework, it doesn't have to be, and I truly hope I can show you that. As Dr Chloe Farahar says in *The Neurodiversity Reader*:

> The pathology paradigm framing trauma responses to a disordered society as 'illnesses' is only one narrative to explain psychologically-divergent experience, neurodiversity is another. The former has dehumanized, and physically and chemically incarcerated those with different neurologies, different responses to trauma. The latter, if given the chance, can free the same people, yet still offer real, human support to those whose psychologies have tried to protect them in ways that society struggles to understand or accept.[21]

---

21 Chloe Farahar, 'Stigmaphrenia: Reducing Mental Health Stigma with a Script about Neurodiversity', in *The Neurodiversity Reader: Exploring Concepts, Lived Experience and Implications for Practice*, ed. Damian Milton (Shoreham by Sea: Pavilion Publishing and Media, 2020).

It's time to give the Neurodiversity Paradigm a chance. It's time to give people a chance. The Pathology Paradigm says neurodivergent individuals like ourselves are broken and wrong for existing, and we should really get on top of that, while the Neurodiversity Paradigm says we aren't broken or wrong for simply being different, and we shouldn't jump towards 'cure' and 'treatment' as the default response. We are simply saying that we don't actually need to call someone 'disordered' when the goal is to support someone to thrive with positive well-being. That's why we need this shift, but in order for this shift to happen, we need to have an understanding of what the Neurodiversity Paradigm actually is.

CHAPTER 5

The Neurodiversity Paradigm

In order to understand the Neurodiversity Paradigm, it's important to understand it is a lens through which we view neurodiversity and understand neurodivergence, which means we need to recognize what both neurodiversity and neurodivergent mean.

In the 1990s, Judy Singer introduced the term 'neurodiversity' in her dissertation and defined it as 'a subset of biodiversity [which] refers to the virtually infinite neuro-cognitive variability within Earth's human population. It points to the fact that every human has a unique nervous system with a unique combination of abilities and needs.'[1]

Basically, neurodiversity names a biological reality and refers to the natural diversity of human minds. It is a fact that we are diverse in our minds and ways of existing, just as we are diverse in our ethnicity, culture, religion, gender and sexuality. While neurodiversity refers to the whole of humanity, neurodivergent specifically refers to individuals who diverge from dominant societal norms – otherwise known as the individuals who have been labelled with a disorder by the Pathology Paradigm.

1   Judy Singer, *Neurodiversity: The Birth of an Idea* (Lexington, KY: Judy Singer, 2017).

Neurodiversity is a part of human diversity, and just as Western society has tried to extinguish other forms of human diversity, the Pathology Paradigm aims to extinguish neurodiversity by labelling certain ways of existing as abnormal, unnatural and disordered. As you would've seen in the previous chapter, Western society has tried to extinguish other forms of human diversity under the guise of the Pathology Paradigm, too. As Dr Nick Walker emphasizes:

> The social dynamics that manifest in regard to neurodiversity are similar to the social dynamics that manifest in regard to other forms of human diversity (e.g., diversity of race, culture, gender, or sexual orientation). These dynamics include the dynamics of social power relations – the dynamics of social inequality, privilege, and oppression – as well as the dynamics by which diversity, when embraced, acts as a source of creative potential within a group or society.[2]

The Pathology Paradigm is not friendly to any form of human diversity, and it both harms and oppresses everyone.

That's why we need to stop viewing human diversity through the lens of the Pathology Paradigm. We need a new lens, a lens that recognizes neurodiversity. This is where the Neurodiversity Paradigm comes in. It is about fostering and respecting the diversity of all brains and minds. It's an alternative lens or framework for understanding differences and distress. It's why the Neurodiversity Paradigm is meaningful and liberating for everyone, not just neurodivergent individuals. This framework also has practical benefits that can create a culture shift. I really want people to know that everything I'm about to suggest and propose has the sole purpose of ensuring no individual ever feels as though they are broken or

---

2   Nick Walker, *Neuroqueer Heresies: Notes on the Neurodiversity Paradigm, Autistic Empowerment, and Postnormal Possibilities* (Fort Worth, TX: Autonomous Press, 2021).

wrong. I think it's a lonely thing to believe you're broken, and it changes how you see yourself and how you move through the world – as if you are separate from it, never quite fitting in. It is what disorder succeeds in accomplishing: othering us and separating us. And we feel it, we live it.

Understanding the Neurodiversity Paradigm

Let's do a quick refresher on what a paradigm and paradigm shift is. A paradigm is simply a name for a set of principles, ideas or assumptions that provides a framework for how we view, interpret or understand something. When we talk about a paradigm shift, we're talking about changing how we view or understand something. In this case, we're talking about how we view and understand neurodiversity and neurodivergent individuals. You might be wondering why a paradigm shift is necessary or even helpful, and it's because neurodivergent individuals have only ever been viewed through the dominant framework – the Pathology Paradigm – and this is what has led to individuals being labelled as disordered or broken. If we want to change how people view neurodivergent individuals, we want a paradigm shift and we want the Neurodiversity Paradigm.

While Judy Singer introduced the term 'neurodiversity', it was Dr Nick Walker, an Autistic scholar, who proposed the idea of the Neurodiversity Paradigm. While the Neurodiversity Movement was making strides in social and political advocacy, there was still a need for a paradigm shift if we wanted to ensure our well-being. In a way, this paradigm shift is actually quite similar to the shift in how the LGBTQIA+ community was once viewed. As you know, homosexuality was once labelled as a disorder and viewed as abnormal or unhealthy, but thanks to the hard work and advocacy of the community, it was removed from the DSM and no longer seen as a disorder. By recognizing homosexuality for what it was – sexual diversity

- there was a shift towards acceptance and inclusion. The Neurodiversity Paradigm argues for this same acceptance and inclusion!

Like all paradigms, there is a group of ideas or principles behind the framework, and while Dr Nick Walker has done some incredible work developing the fundamental principles in conjunction with the community, it is my aim to expand on these principles. By doing that, I also hope to address some common concerns and criticisms that people have in regard to the Neurodiversity Paradigm.

Principle 1: Neurodiversity is a natural and valuable form of human diversity

The Neurodiversity Paradigm recognizes neurodiversity as a natural form of human diversity just like gender diversity, sexual diversity or cultural diversity. Instead of understanding cognitive, emotional, developmental, sensory, behavioural and learning differences as disorders or illnesses, we can understand them as natural variations where one brain or mind is no more right than another. The Neurodiversity Paradigm wants us to see variations in our minds and brains as natural and even as vital as variations in skin colour, gender, sexuality, ability, shape and size. Most importantly, no one has the right to determine what mind or brain should be treated, cured or eradicated, which brings us to the second principle.

Principle 2: There is no such thing as an ideal or normal mind or brain

This is probably the most fundamental idea within the Neurodiversity Paradigm; that there is no perfect ideal of what a human mind or brain should be. The Neurodiversity Paradigm says neurodiversity, the diversity of minds and brains, is a natural thing, and there isn't anything pathological, unhealthy, negative or disordered about neurodivergence. When we think of unhealthy or abnormal minds, we are actually thinking of minds that have been labelled as diverging from dominant cultural and social norms. A normal mind doesn't mean normal, because the idea of a normal mind is as valid as a normal gender, culture, sexuality or ethnicity – and by that I mean it isn't valid at all. If there's no such thing as a normal or ideal mind, there can be no such thing as an abnormal or less-than-ideal mind, which brings us to the next idea underpinning the Neurodiversity Paradigm.

Principle 3: There is no such thing as normal because normal is a social construct

If you look at the definition of 'normal' in the Merriam-Webster dictionary, normal means conforming to a standard.[3] I mean, that's exactly it – normal is merely a social construct that refers to the dominant, colonial, capitalist standards within Western society. It's not actually normal; it's just socially acceptable. As Dr Nick Walker emphasizes, 'the concept of a normal brain or a normal person has no more objective scientific validity – and serves no better purpose – than the concept of a master race'.[4] It is a term used to control us and force us into following these dominant, capitalist and colonial standards and norms. If we can recognize that normal is just a so-cial construct that people in power made up, and we toss the idea of normal out of the window, the concept of disorders can also be tossed out of the window.

Principle 4: Differences are just that – differences – and shouldn't automatically be viewed as the problem when it comes to challenges, difficulties or struggles

It's important to remember that the Neurodiversity Paradigm

---

3   www.merriam-webster.com/dictionary/normal
4   Nick Walker, *Neuroqueer Heresies: Notes on the Neurodiversity Paradigm, Autistic Empowerment, and Postnormal Possibilities* (Fort Worth, TX: Autonomous Press, 2021).

doesn't deny that differences exist and that challenges exist as a result of these differences; rather, we shouldn't assign value judgements of good and bad when it comes to these differences. Similarly, we shouldn't view differences as wrong or right, normal or abnormal; differences are just that – differences. In fact, that's the problem with the Pathology Paradigm: it frames any deviation or any divergence as a moral failing of the individual. That's the problem with framing people's differences or distress as being a result of a disease or illness; it assumes their differences and distress are a problem residing within the individual. Of course, it doesn't mean we ignore difficulties, struggles or challenges. However, it does mean we stop framing individuals who require support or accommodations as abnormal or wrong. It also means we have to stop assuming that it's the differences that are at the root of any challenges or difficulties. Instead of a preoccupation with finding ways to help neurodivergent individuals 'fit in' better, we want to find ways to help society and environments fit neurodivergent individuals better. We go into how we can help society and environments fit neurodivergent individuals in Chapter 9: A Neurodiversity-Affirming Society.

Principle 5: Neurodivergences are not disorders or diseases, but they can be disabilities

I want to make this very clear: being neurodivergent doesn't mean we can't be disabled – it just means we are not broken because of it. In order to understand this, it's important to recognize that the medical model views disability in much the same way as the Pathology Paradigm views disorder: that we are broken and abnormal. When it comes to the social model of disability, however, that acknowledges that we are not broken or abnormal. In fact, disability is a very normal part of human diversity and a normal part of human life. Jennifer Litton Tidd, a restraint and seclusion survivor, shares this in an article on the difference between the medical and social model of disability:

> A social model perspective does not deny the reality of impairment, sickness, nor its impact on the individual, or a caretaker. However, it does challenge the physical, attitudinal, communication, and social environment to accommodate impairment as an expected incident of human diversity. Yes, not only is disability not 'abnormal', it's a very normal part of the human condition. Very few people are born, live their entire lives, and die without experiencing disability.[5]

In a way, I feel that the Neurodiversity Paradigm is reframing disorders through the social model of disability by recognizing them as neurodivergences. While the Pathology Paradigm implies that disorder is inherently negative, the Neurodiversity Paradigm is implying that neurodivergence is neutral. While the Pathology Paradigm frames some needs and differences as abnormal, the Neurodiversity Paradigm frames all needs as normal. At the end of the day, we all have fundamental needs; it's just that some needs have been normalized while other needs have been framed as unreasonable or unnatural. On that note, we need to recognize that individuals have a unique combination of strengths, weaknesses, abilities and needs, where none is framed as more ideal than another.

Principle 6: We do not pathologize or blame people for their responses or experiences of distress

It is deeply rooted in the Pathology Paradigm that distress, both emotional and mental, is a biological defect, a deficit, a disorder. It

---

5   Jennifer Litton Tidd, 'What is the difference between the medical and social models of disability and why does it matter?' Alliance against Seclusion and Restraint, 18 May 2021. https://endseclusion.org/2021/05/18/what-is-the-difference-between-the-medical-and-social-models-of-disability-and-why-does-it-matter

doesn't make sense that we label distress as a disorder, which implies it is dysfunctional, because really it is functional. It is a protest against unmet needs, societal expectations, capitalist standards, oppressive systems and unfair circumstances. If someone breaks their leg, we don't refer to them as someone with a broken bone disorder; we recognize it was a response or reaction to their environment or circumstances. The same applies to distress: it is an individual's response or reaction to their environment, and there is nothing abnormal about that. In fact, it isn't the individual and their responses or distress that is abnormal; it is the circumstances that led to the distress that is actually abnormal. Dr James Davies shared this quote on Twitter that I believe is extremely relevant to this particular principle: 'to demedicalize distress is not to delegitimize distress. One can honor, respect and care for profound suffering without labelling it as illness, pathology or disorder.'[6]

When we pathologize and reduce someone's responses and distress to a disorder, the individual is shouldering all the blame. It is a very specific tactic with the goal to uphold capitalist and colonial norms and standards because at the end of the day, like Dr Ayesha Khan has said, 'if people are manipulated into thinking the root cause of their mental distress is biological defects or chemical imbalances, then they'd never identify the oppressive systems that are slowly killing them as the cause of their suffering'.[7]

In order to move away from the Pathology Paradigm and towards the Neurodiversity Paradigm, we need new ways of understanding, respecting and supporting individuals who are

6   Dr James Davies PhD (@JDaviesPhD), 'To demedicalise distress is not to delegitimise distress. one can honor, respect and care for profound suffering without labeling it as illness, pathology or disorder', Twitter, 17 January 2021. https://twitter.com/jdaviesphd/status/1350631426941714440
7   Dr Ayesha Khan (@wokescientist). 'A little note on my main criticisms of mainstream mental health systems under capitalism', Instagram, 28 April 2022. www.instagram.com/p/CfUaW7Huacf

experiencing distress without pathologizing them or blaming them. I would like to make two suggestions in regard to this: the first is that we truly need to learn from non-Western understandings of distress and suffering (which, as a white person, I cannot speak on) and the second suggestion is adopting the Power Threat Meaning Framework as a non-pathologizing and alternative way of understanding distress, emotions and experiences.

The Power Threat Meaning Framework (PTMF) was co-authored by psychologists and individuals with lived experience and it moves away from asking 'what is wrong with you?' and moves towards asking 'what happened to you?', which is significant because people don't exist in a vacuum; our distress doesn't occur in a vacuum. The PTMF explores how systems and structures impact our lives from housing, money, education, relationships and resources - our access to these as well as our lack of them. Similarly, it also explores the messages we receive about how we should act, how we should feel, how we should look, how we should behave and how we should function. Basically, the PTMF shows how distress can be understood in the context of our circumstances and environments as well as the expectations and norms of the society we live in.[8] While this framework may not work for every single individual, it is an alternative framework to consider and use.

Principle 7: We respect the autonomy of individuals in defining their own meanings around their experiences

We cannot have the Neurodiversity Paradigm replicating the Pathology Paradigm, which is why we cannot do what the Pathology Paradigm does - defining and labelling people's experiences for them. We need to respect the autonomy of individuals when it comes

---

8 Mary Boyle and Lucy Johnstone, *A Straight Talking Introduction to the Power Threat Meaning Framework* (Monmouth: PCCS Books, 2020).

to how they identify and how they talk about or define their own experiences, differences and distress. In other words, we need to recognize that individuals are the experts of their own experiences.

I've been talking about how mental health conditions count as neurodivergent, both online and within my advocacy work, for a while now. 'Most people with mental health conditions lack insight into their state, traits or experiences' is a common narrative or argument that I've come across when it comes to recognizing various mental health conditions as neurodivergent. Within the field of psychiatry, and if we follow the Pathology Paradigm, having insight means you can acknowledge your mental illness or mental disorder and your need for treatment. If we follow the Neurodiversity Paradigm, we need to recognize that individuals have the right to define their own experiences, which means we cannot automatically accuse an individual of lacking insight. In fact, I've yet to find an argument for lack of insight that isn't defined by agreeableness or compliance with the Pathology Paradigm, because the concept of insight relies on the assumption that the provider or professional always knows best.

If someone doesn't recognize their experiences as a mental illness, disorder or deficit, is it actually because they're lacking insight or is it because their understanding of their experience simply doesn't align with the Pathology Paradigm? If someone doesn't want to take medication for their schizophrenia or bipolar, is it actually because they're lacking insight or is it because they don't view their neurodivergence as needing to be treated, cured or fixed? If someone doesn't view their experiences of hearing voices as distressing, is it actually because of a lack of insight or is it because someone can hear voices without finding it distressing? When the concept of insight was first introduced within psychiatry, it was defined as a correct attitude towards the significant change within oneself, and it's really important to remember that psychiatry's idea of a correct attitude is an attitude that abides by the Pathology Paradigm. If we want to follow the Neurodiversity Paradigm, we need to recognize that the provider or professional doesn't always know best; it's the individual who actually knows best.

If we move towards considering individuals as the experts of their own experiences, we also need to remember that individuals have the right to choose how they define themselves, too. If we consider identity-first language and person-first language, for example, there is a strong consensus in the Autistic community that we prefer identity-first language such as 'Autistic person' over person-first language such as 'person with Autism spectrum disorder', but there are also individuals who fall outside the consensus. Either way, their right to choose and self-define also matters, so it comes down to respecting what the community says they prefer in regard to language while also respecting each individual and their right to self-define and choose.

We also need to make room for individuals to define success for themselves. Too often, we assume success means working full-time or success means independence, and that simply isn't a reality for everyone, but it doesn't mean we are wrong or broken for not achieving this.

We also need to make room for individuals to define what is functional or dysfunctional for them because, too often, we associate functional with a very narrow set of standards and expectations. Functional means something that works well while dysfunctional means something that doesn't work well. As someone with ADHD, I tend to work well when I am able to work in an environment that suits me and I can complete tasks and projects in a non-linear way, but if you put me in an environment like a workplace where there are different expectations and rules, I don't tend to work as well. Perhaps what is functional and dysfunctional really depends on our environment and the expectations of that environment. We can also apply the same kind of thinking to distress: what is distressing for one person may not be distressing for another person.

Akiko Hart, who wrote a very balanced critique on anti-psychiatry, said something very insightful, and it has stuck with me ever since:

> Once we opt for a single story around mental health, whether that's the story of illness, or the story of trauma, then we by definition exclude others. Arguing that all distress stems from trauma and adversity might not speak to those who experience their distress as spiritual renewal; those who see it as neurodiversity, as part of who they are and how they are in the world; those who understand it as a psychosocial disability; and of course those who see madness as an illness, a sickness of the brain. Many of us will probably see themselves in some or all of these stories, a patchwork of identities. Some of us won't make sense of our distress. That's OK too. There are in fact as many stories as there are people. The single story, whether that of illness or that of trauma, doesn't honour this multiplicity and this complexity.[9]

I have to admit something; I used to be the type of person who would argue and try to convince people on social media that they were neurodivergent and they didn't have a disorder despite their insistence that they viewed it as a disorder. As I look back, I can see that I was doing the exact same thing that psychiatry and the DSM do; forcing a label on to someone and defining their experiences for them. The Neurodiversity Paradigm must not replicate the

9   Jill Anderson, 'Pursuing choice, not truth: Debates around diagnosis in mental health by Akiko Hart', *Asylum Magazine*, 22 June 2018. https://asylummagazine.org/2018/06/pursuing-choice-not-truth-debates-around-diagnosis-in-mental-health-by-akiko-hart

Pathology Paradigm; we cannot be defining people's experiences for them or labelling people's experiences for them.

Principle 8: Everyone deserves personal agency in how we choose to work with our brains

When it comes to adopting the Neurodiversity Paradigm, there's a common concern where individuals worry that the Neurodiversity Paradigm is arguing against any treatment or help whatsoever, and I hope this principle can demonstrate that this isn't the case at all.

What the Neurodiversity Paradigm is arguing for is to not jump to a default pathologization of an individual but instead to recognize that everyone deserves agency in how they choose to work with their brain in addition to defining what is meaningful, functional and distressing. In addition to all that, we need to make sure we don't make the knee-jerk assumption that the individual is the problem: we need to explore and consider everything, from their environment to expectations. You never know, if we adjusted and adapted environments and expectations, maybe some people will have less of a need for medication.

There are always going to be multiple courses of action when it comes to supporting an individual. For some individuals and their neurodivergence, the preferred course of action will be accessing medication if the individual chooses it and if it benefits them. For some individuals and their neurodivergence, the preferred course of action will be providing adjustments and accommodations within their physical environment. For some individuals and their neurodivergence, the preferred course of action will be teaching skills and strategies that work with their brain rather than against their brain. And, of course, for some individuals and their neurodivergence, the preferred course of action will be all three. It's also important to remember that an individual has the right to change their mind and choose alternative courses of action as they see fit.

Kassiane, the creator of the term 'neurodivergent', has shared on Twitter previously how they treat their epilepsy because it benefits them – it is their choice and it still counts as neurodivergent. While many individuals view their seizures as a pathology, something that is unwanted, there are cultures who view seizures as a spiritual practice. I have ADHD, and while I don't believe my ADHD needs fixing or even treating, there have been periods of my life where I've chosen to take medication because it's been beneficial for me. Studying for my postgraduate degree was one of them and, yes, writing this book was another. I've made the choice to take medication, despite not believing for one second that I have deficits, because there are standards and norms (and deadlines) that society expects us to meet. As much as I adjust my lifestyle and external environments around how I work, sometimes I need to work in environments outside of my control that expect me to work a certain way; medication helps me meet the expectations of the environment. Basically, we can't assume everyone experiences or views their neurodivergence the same way.

I believe a big part of this requires us to adjust our understanding of recovery. When it comes to mental health and psychiatric diagnoses like BPD or bipolar, recovery is often defined as learning how to live well.[10] While it's often associated with no longer having any 'symptoms', Mind Australia acknowledges that recovery can be about reclaiming our right to a better life regardless of whether 'symptoms' or, as I prefer to call them, 'traits' are present.[11] If we consider recovery through the lens of the Neurodiversity Paradigm, individuals have the right to define what recovery looks like for them.

10 'Recovery', Mind Australia, 8 September 2022. www.mindaustralia.org.au/resources/recovery
11 'Recovery', Mind Australia, 8 September 2022. www.mindaustralia.org.au/resources/recovery

I think it's important to recognize that recovery doesn't have to be about conforming to neuronormativity or becoming neurotypical if we don't want it to. Perhaps recovery is more about reducing our distress and accommodating our differences rather than changing who we are. If we consider the example of recovery and BPD, I'm always going to have a fear of abandonment and I'm always going to feel super intensely. Sure, I can learn ways to regulate my emotions and I can learn ways to manage the fear, but the fear will always be present and I'm still going to feel intensely. I can reduce the distress and I can find ways to accommodate the differences, but I'm never going to recover in the sense of living without these differences, without these traits.

Similarly, I think it's also important to recognize that recovery shouldn't have to mean getting to the point where we can work a full-time job or remain independent without needing the support of others. While this may be a goal for some individuals, it shouldn't be a blanket goal for everyone. In fact, perhaps recovery should be reframed as discovery because we are discovering what works for us; we are discovering what living our best life looks like for us.

Principle 9: We must recognize intersectionality when it comes to neurodivergence

If our understanding of neurodivergence and neurodiversity only focuses on a white understanding of neurodivergence and neuro-diversity, our understanding is incomplete. If we continue to centre white experiences of neurodivergence, we are leaving out individuals who don't meet this standard, who don't fit our white narrative. We need to stop viewing someone's experiences, traits and characteristics in the context of Western society, of whiteness, because if we don't recognize the intersection of race, disability, gender and sexuality when it comes to neurodivergence, we also end up creating more barriers and more unfair standards and norms.

I've listed and defined some principles, but it might be helpful to know how we can actually apply these principles. The Neurodiversity Paradigm isn't just a bunch of ideals or principles but a paradigm for everyone to adopt on a personal level as well as on a wider level within our communities, workplaces and classrooms. It is an alternative to how society currently understands any individual with differences, and there are many practical applications that we can implement to create a better environment for *all* individuals.

Applying these principles

Shifting our language

When it comes to a paradigm shift, our language is very important because it reflects the lens we are using and the principles we are upholding. If you're a mental health professional or any kind of helping professional, it's important to recognize and challenge the language within the Pathology Paradigm while moving towards more neurodiversity-affirming language. As Dr Nick Walker explains in her article, 'Throw away the master's tools', 'the shift from the Pathology Paradigm to the Neurodiversity Paradigm calls for a radical shift in language, because the appropriate language for discussing medical problems is quite different from the appropriate language for discussing diversity'.[12]

One way we can shift our language is by challenging deficit-based language which is rooted within the Pathology Paradigm. Using deficit language reinforces the idea of normal, which doesn't actually exist, because it implies we are lacking something or missing something that separates us from normal. If we shift our language

---

12 Nick Walker, *Neuroqueer Heresies: Notes on the Neurodiversity Paradigm, Autistic Empowerment, and Postnormal Possibilities* (Fort Worth, TX: Autonomous Press, 2021).

towards the Neurodiversity Paradigm, we can acknowledge that neurotypical people are not the benchmark for normality, so therefore deficits do not exist. I think it's important to realize that deficit language impacts neurodivergent individuals through how we view ourselves as well as how society views us. By labelling our differences and needs as a deficit, it often means our needs will be seen as a burden rather than just human needs.

EXAMPLES OF HOW WE CAN SHIFT OUR LANGUAGE ⬇

Instead of using this:	Use this:
Disorder or illness	Disability or neurodivergence
Deficit	Difference
Symptoms	Traits, experiences, responses, characteristics
High-functioning or low-functioning	Low level of support or high level of support
Normal	Dominant standards and expectations or neuronormative
Problem	Challenge or difficulty
Attention seeking	Support seeking
Obsessions	Deep interests or intense interests
Comorbidity*	Co-occurring or co-existing

* Shifting from the Pathology Paradigm towards a Neurodiversity Paradigm means moving away from pathologizing language. As comorbidity is a medical term to describe the existence of more than one disease or illness, it's important that we replace this term with one that isn't rooted in the disease model.

Supporting neurodivergent individuals

As the Neurodiversity Paradigm is an alternative framework to the Pathology Paradigm and exists in opposition to the Pathology Paradigm, it is significantly useful and necessary for psychiatrists, psychologists, social workers, therapists, speech pathologists, occupational therapists and other providers to adopt and utilize in their practice. When we shift from the pathology lens to a neurodiversity lens, it requires changing how we view individuals as well as ourselves. It requires shifting how we understand individuals, and it requires approaching difficulties, challenges and distress with curiosity, compassion and collaboration. I totally recognize that it's not easy shifting from a pathology lens to a neurodiversity lens, but maybe I can make the process easier by showing what it actually looks like when we do support individuals using a neurodiversity lens. I've tried to do just that in the table below by comparing the Pathology Paradigm and the Neurodiversity Paradigm so that providers will be able to recognize where they can challenge and adjust their practice accordingly.

PATHOLOGY PARADIGM VERSUS NEURODIVERSITY PARADIGM – SUMMARY

Pathology paradigm	Neurodiversity paradigm
Ideal outcome is compliance	Ideal outcome is autonomy
Relies on typical and neuronormative goals, expectations, functioning and milestones	Respects individual goals, needs and differences
Spoken communication is seen as superior and associated with ability to think	All forms of communication are seen as valid and competence is presumed
Labels behaviour based on external observations	Seeks to understand the thoughts, feelings and context behind behaviours

Reducing symptoms	Reducing distress, accommodating traits/differences
Reducing distress, accommodating traits/differences	Functioning is self-defined
Worth equates ability and productivity	Everyone is worthy
Success and productivity are measured by capitalist and Western societal standards	Success is self-defined and productivity is not a requirement or expectation
Reinforces binary ways of thinking e.g. right/wrong, normal/abnormal	Focuses on what is meaningful and recognizes there is no such thing as normal
Supporting individuals revolves only around changing their behaviour and traits	Allowing individuals to determine how they would like to work with their neurodivergence
Encouraging only self-regulation and independence	Encourages self-regulation and independence as well as interdependence and co-regulation

I recognize it can be hard shifting from the Pathology Paradigm to the Neurodiversity Paradigm, especially when the Pathology Paradigm has been our dominant framework for so long – for most of you, it is probably the only paradigm you've ever known or ever been taught. I also want to express that shifting to a new paradigm, a new framework, is never instant; it requires constant reflection, awareness, unlearning and relearning. While it might be difficult, it doesn't make it any less worthwhile. It's my hope that every provider can start supporting their clients through the Neurodiversity Paradigm rather than the Pathology Paradigm, which is why I've written some reflections to help providers on this learning journey.

O O O

REFLECTIONS FOR PROVIDERS ⬇

Am I allowing neurodivergent individuals to define their own goals and outcomes when it comes to therapy?

- Am I allowing neurodivergent individuals to define their own meanings and expectations when it comes to success, recovery and functioning?

- Am I giving neurodivergent individuals the space to create their own meanings around their experiences?

- Am I respecting and accommodating all the multiple forms of communication, expression, movement, feeling and functioning, and how am I applying this within my practice?

- In what ways can I improve the accessibility of my environment and practice as well as my website and forms?

- How am I affirming and understanding the different ways of being that are often stigmatized such as hearing voices, having alters or experiencing manic episodes?

- Am I challenging the concept of independence as the ideal goal or outcome within my practice?

- How can I provide accommodations, tools and alternative ways of doing things to suit someone's executive functioning differences rather than increasing executive function skills?

- How am I challenging social norms and expectations that neurodivergent individuals are expected to meet and conform to? Am I challenging how we define ideal or normal functioning?

- Am I considering how community, belonging, acceptance and co-regulation are important parts of well-being alongside the traditional domains of employment, education and living?

The future of research

I want to mention another part of society that seriously needs to adopt the Neurodiversity Paradigm, and that's the field of research. We desperately need research to shift towards following the Neurodiversity Paradigm more than anything because way too much research is based on the Pathology Paradigm where outcomes focus on fixing us, making us more normal and defining our experiences for us. If researchers could apply the principles of the Neurodiversity Paradigm, it would shift the outcomes and objectives of research, and perhaps we can focus more on finding ways to support our differences, human experiences, ways of being and functioning.

An important aspect of research adopting the Neurodiversity Paradigm is that neurodivergent individuals will have a say in what is researched as well as why and how. When neurodivergent individuals are left out of research about us, the research is incomplete. The research isn't accurate because it's judging us from the outside and it's making assumptions based on what is observed rather than our internal experiences. Put simply, research doesn't listen to us. If the research community was truly concerned about our well-being, it would start allowing neurodivergent individuals to have a say in the what, why and how, when it comes to research. Instead of focusing on how to prevent Autism, research should be focusing on how to support Autistic individuals. Instead of research focusing on how to treat ADHD, research should be focusing on how to support and accommodate our differences.

O O O

APPLYING THE PRINCIPLES OF THE ⬇ NEURODIVERSITY PARADIGM TO RESEARCH

- Actively seeking out the views of neurodivergent individuals to make informed decisions about what research is needed and valuable.

- Shifting the language within research as well as changing how research describes and discusses neurodivergent individuals.

- Using strength-based language as well as identity-first language rather than deficit language.

- Partnering with neurodivergent individuals with research about us as well as allowing more neurodivergent individuals to lead discussions and research about us.

- Focusing on challenges and barriers within society and exploring accessibility and accommodations that benefit neurodivergent individuals rather than defaulting to viewing them as people with a problem to be fixed or changed.

When it comes to the Neurodiversity Paradigm, it isn't just a framework for providers, professionals or researchers; it's also a framework for society. It's a framework for everyone. While I know the Neurodiversity Paradigm has been adopted by many providers when it comes to Autism, ADHD and learning disabilities, I want to see providers support all neurodivergent individuals when it comes to following the Neurodiversity Paradigm. I truly believe the Neurodiversity Paradigm is a way for society to change how they view and understand differences and neurodivergent individuals. I believe the Neurodiversity Paradigm is an opportunity to stop othering differences by challenging the current dominant norms and accepting the human spectrum of communicating, feeling, thinking, expressing, focusing, functioning and socializing. I believe the Neurodiversity Paradigm is an opportunity for individuals to accept themselves instead of viewing themselves as broken, abnormal, wrong or disordered. I believe the Neurodiversity Paradigm is how we begin to acknowledge and appreciate the diversity of being human.

NEURODIVERGENT UMBRELLA*

ADHD	DID & OSDD	BIPOLAR	AUTISM
ASPD	NPD	EPILEPSY	GAD
DYSLEXIA	BPD	OCD	ABI/TBI
DYSPRAXIA	CPTSD	TIC DISORDERS	
PTSD	HSP	SCHIZOPHRENIA	
SENSORY PROCESSING		MISOPHONIA	HPD
DYSCALCULIA		DOWN SYNDROME	
DYSGRAPHIA		FASD	SYNESTHESIA

*Non-exhaustive list
www.livedexperienceeducator.com | @livedexperienceeducator

CHAPTER 6

The Neurodivergent Umbrella

In the year 2000, Kassiane Asasumasu, who is a biracial and multiply neurodivergent advocate and activist, coined the term 'neurodivergent', and because there is often confusion, I want to remind everyone that neurodivergent is a separate term to neurodiversity, which was coined by Judy Singer. If there is one thing to know about the term 'neurodivergent', it is that it is an inclusive and value-neutral term to describe any divergence from dominant societal standards and norms and it includes much, much more than Autism and ADHD. I would like to share with you an infographic I created a while ago – the neurodivergent umbrella – and invite you to take a moment to see what counts as neurodivergent.

I imagine there are a number of different responses to this; you may be surprised, you may be confused or you may even feel a little bit angry. On the other hand, there may even be people who feel seen for the first time or feel as if they're a part of something. I've witnessed every one of those responses when I have talked about how neurodivergent includes all of those things above (and more) online. There are other interpretations of the term 'neurodivergent', where some individuals believe it only refers to individuals with neurological conditions. Some individuals believe it only refers to innate conditions that are an inherent part of someone's identity such as Autism or ADHD. I do believe the confusion, disbelief and even denial of the inclusion of mental health conditions isn't the fault of an individual. There's not enough written material out there that really unpacks what neurodivergent means, which is where the misinterpretation comes from. It's my hope that this chapter can fill that gap. In order to understand why neurodivergent includes things from neurodevelopmental conditions to psychiatric conditions to neurological conditions to mental illnesses, there are some important things to know that may clear up any confusion.

It is a term that includes innate neurodivergence or acquired/developed neurodivergence

I'll often read comments by people saying they weren't born this way, so how on earth can they be neurodivergent? The thing is, neurodivergence has nothing to do with how you came to diverge, but it has everything to do with the fact that you do diverge now. When it comes to neurodivergence, it can be innate or it can be acquired or developed – and more often than not, it's a combination of the two. Often, people assume if something is neurodivergent, it's something you were born with, which means you wouldn't want to heal it or change it. However, just because something is acquired or developed later in life, it doesn't necessarily mean it is something an individual wants to heal, change or cure.

Some examples of innate neurodivergences are:

- Autism
- ADHD
- dyslexia.

Examples of acquired neurodivergences are:

- complex post-traumatic stress disorder (CPTSD)
- obsessive-compulsive disorder (OCD)
- acquired brain injury
- borderline personality disorder (BPD).

Some individuals, including myself, believe categorizing neurodivergence as innate or acquired serves little purpose in understanding neurodivergence. These categorizations aren't as clear-cut as we make them out to be, because there is a significant overlap between many of them. As an example, both bipolar and schizophrenia are often acquired later in life, but there are studies that reveal a genetic component; they're both acquired and innate. As I like to say, it doesn't matter how you come to diverge; it matters that you do diverge.

It is an umbrella term
I've had people ask me in the past, 'If both Autism and ADHD are under the umbrella with mental illnesses, what's stopping them from seeing Autism as a mental illness?', which is a valid concern, so I like to compare it to the umbrella term 'queer'. As you may or may not know, 'queer' is an umbrella term for any identity that isn't straight or cisgender. If you're gay, you can identify as queer. If you're trans, you can identify as queer. If you're pansexual, you can identify as queer. In fact, even if you don't identify with a specific sexuality or gender and you prefer to keep it vague, you can identify as queer. Just because someone identifies as queer, it doesn't mean that every single person has the same sexuality or gender.

It's the same for neurodivergent; it's an umbrella term for anyone who diverges from dominant societal norms; it doesn't specifically say what our experiences or differences are other than the fact that we simply do diverge. It's an umbrella term for all the ways we may diverge from the way we think, feel, learn, communicate, behave and function.

It is a neutral term, not a negative term nor is it a positive term

It is not a positive term where it's all sunshine and superpowers. It is a neutral term that describes someone who diverges – that's literally it. It refers to someone whose mind or functioning diverges from dominant societal norms, standards and expectations. And there are so many ways we can diverge.

It's a common misconception that neurodivergence must mean something positive, so I wanted to share my personal relationship with bipolar. We don't have to view our bipolar as a friend, but we don't have to view our bipolar as the enemy either; perhaps we can view our bipolar as a neutral companion throughout our lives. I live with bipolar and experience predominantly a mix of manic and hypomanic episodes, and while I can't begin to describe the consequences and distress that have come from my manic episodes in the past, I also believe that these episodes would have come with fewer consequences and less distress if I was able to work with them instead of against them, with more accommodations and support.

I'm not saying my bipolar is a superpower, as some people assume when they hear the word 'neurodivergent', and I don't necessarily view it as positive, but I also don't view it as negative either. I view my bipolar and manic episodes as a difference – a difference that means I experience a change in energy, emotions, thinking, behaviours and perception of time. It isn't that I would wish bipolar on anyone, but I also wouldn't return it either. If I'm honest, I see my bipolar as a part of me – as natural and inevitable, like my hair colour and eye colour. As you know, neurodiversity means variation is neither good nor bad; it just is. If we apply it to bipolar, we aren't saying bipolar is super awesome; it's just acknowledging that it's another difference in the way we experience life – or, more specifically, the way we experience shifts in moods, energy and our perception of time. Every individual deserves the opportunity to define their own traits or experiences. If someone wants to view their bipolar as a neutral companion, they can. If someone wants to view their bipolar as a strength because it comes with creativity, energy and great ideas, they can.

It isn't a term that only refers to neurodivergences we do not want to cure or treat

There's often an assumption in online discourse that neurodivergent refers to natural variations that we don't want to change, treat or cure, and I really want to challenge this because it isn't true at all. As soon as someone's functioning falls outside societal standards and expectations – such as hearing voices, experiencing manic episodes, experiencing seizures, experiencing executive functioning differences – that is neurodivergent. You can be neurodivergent and you can take medication to prevent manic episodes. You can be neurodivergent and you can want to get rid of your seizures. You can be neurodivergent and you can view your differences as natural differences that can't be changed with medication but only accommodated. You can be neurodivergent and you can view your differences as distressing. Basically, neurodivergent isn't a term that assigns a value judgement to our differences and experiences. It is a neutral term that gives us the autonomy to determine how we want to work with our brains instead of society assuming what we may want or need.

It is an identity you can choose if the shoe fits

One of the most important things to recognize about the term 'neurodivergent', is that it is a social identity, not a clinical term, medical term or another diagnosis. Neurodivergent means that the way I function diverges from the way society expects me to function, and that it doesn't mean there's anything wrong with me. While it can and does present challenges and difficulties, this doesn't actually mean there is anything inherently abnormal about me. Identifying as neurodivergent means being able to understand, address and accept the challenges you might've faced in life without having to view yourself as the problem. It's a lens through which you can understand your differences and needs, and that you move through this world and function differently.

I believe it's incredibly important to recognize how this identity, this lens, applies to individuals who live with mental health conditions. If someone who is neurotypical experiences emotional states in a relatively linear progression, someone who is neurodivergent would diverge from a stable, linear emotional state and experience emotional states that are less linear. Sound familiar? I've just described someone with bipolar. I've described myself, actually! See, the way I experience moods diverges from how someone else experiences moods. It is an extreme, but it's not inherently bad or wrong. While it has the potential to be distressing and sometimes even harmful for an individual, it doesn't mean an individual is wrong, bad or even disordered. We can provide support to an individual without viewing them as such. If neurodivergent is to have a mind that works differently where your functioning diverges from dominant societal norms and expectations, someone who experiences mania would qualify.

If you feel that 'neurodivergent' describes your experiences, you can identify as neurodivergent. You get to choose if you're neurodivergent. It's not a label someone else can force upon you and it's not a label someone can take away from you or deny you. It's your choice. If you would rather view your experiences and your differences as a disorder, that is up to you, but if you would rather view your experiences and your differences as neurodivergent, it's right here for you to embrace.

Personal stories

If you're new to understanding the importance of using the term 'neurodivergent', you might be wondering what the point of it all is, or you might even be wondering why it actually matters, and that's totally fine, as long as you're willing to listen. Identifying as neuro-divergent can have a significant impact on how we see ourselves.

When it comes to viewing ourselves as either having a disorder or being neurodivergent, it can be the difference between hating ourselves and loving ourselves, and I truly believe no one should move through life hating themselves. I don't expect you to take my word for it, though, which is why I decided to ask neurodivergent individuals to share what identifying as neurodivergent means for them and what kind of difference it has made in their lives. I feel honoured to share these stories with you and I hope these stories can demonstrate how identifying as neurodivergent can create a positive change.

'I'm not broken, I'm different'

Aiden shares how identifying as neurodivergent has helped him re-alize he's not a problem:

> I used to hate myself for all the things I did that were 'differ-ent', I especially loathed the person who I was before I started intensely masking. I thought I was the only one acting like this and that I was making problems for other people, but now I've learned that I'm simply neurodivergent. This epiphany has com-pletely altered how I view myself. I no longer hate who I used to be, but now I feel sorrow for all the anger he faced from himself and others by existing. Discovering I'm neurodivergent helped me realize I'm not a problem, and that my behaviour is

normal for *me*. I understand myself, and now, instead of hiding my needs, I am beginning to feel like I deserve to feel like I can thrive and get the accommodations I need to do so.

Karina, on identifying as neurodivergent, shares this:

It has helped me understand myself and provided a sense of relief that I'm a whole neurodivergent person functioning as my brain intends, instead of always feeling like a broken person.

Ren also shares how identifying as neurodivergent has helped them reframe and destigmatize their entire outlook on how their brain works and how it's helpful and healing:

I no longer always feel like a 'broken' neurotypical person who just can't function well enough, and I can far more easily identify areas that I genuinely would like to improve in and would like to change about myself, and what are simply symptoms of my neurodivergence that I am allowed to live with as is, without shame or self-hatred.

Martha shares this wonderful reflection on identifying as neurodivergent and how society is neurodiverse so we shouldn't expect everyone to be neurotypical:

Before identifying as neurodivergent, I felt like I just have these illnesses that I can do nothing about. Neurodiversity made me understand that people have different needs and that my symptoms can be softer when I honour my needs, rather than ignore them, while trying to do what everyone else is doing. I experience everyday life differently from the norm. I have other needs and energy levels than what society depicts as normal. The term 'neurodivergent' allows me to feel valid with my needs, rather than sick/not belonging.

Em, who has bipolar and identifies as neurodivergent, shares this:

It helps others and ourselves to understand that there is nothing inherently 'wrong' with us, but our brains are just built differently. This means that we no longer have to keep fighting to get back to that 'normal' person state and keep guilting ourselves for not being 'normal', instead understanding that we exist on a spectrum and it's normal and okay to fluctuate on that spectrum in our own way. It's taken me a long time to come to this realization, but since reframing this mindset, I have come to terms with so much more about myself than I ever have before.

'I'm no longer fixing myself, I'm accommodating myself'
Izzy, who has always felt as if they weren't trying hard enough, shares this:

I was pressured my whole life to improve and change in ways that weren't possible for me, and pushed to do things the way neurotypical people do. If I could do it that way, then it was 'success', and if I couldn't, then I wasn't trying hard enough. Now I feel like I can find ways to make the world work for me. I don't have to change for the world. And now I can feel like there are people who are just like me.

Fee views neurodivergence as the overarching lens through which they see, process and think about the world, and shares this:

I no longer feel angry at myself or guilty for not being able to do things that come naturally to others. Instead, I am able to understand why that is, which also helps me to manage other people's expectations about what I 'should' and 'shouldn't' be able to do. Regardless of whether they wish to accept that as the truth or concede to what I have told them, I am happy that I can be honest about my capacity on any given day. Identifying as neurodivergent has provided a language that allows me to advocate for myself. I also no longer spend hours ruminating about what is 'wrong' with me and now accept myself for who I am, while still working on the things I'd like to get better at.

Maia, an ADHDer, shares this:

It's allowed me a language to give myself permission to stop holding myself to neurotypical standards and think outside the box – it created space to advocate for altering my environment and expectations instead of focusing on 'fixing' myself to fit someone else's definition of functioning.

Anna shows how identifying as neurodivergent is about working with yourself instead of against yourself:

It shifted my perspective to understanding what my needs, challenges and strengths are, and playing to them. Rather than trying to 'do it like I'm supposed to', actually making my life liveable, comfortable, accessible and enjoyable for me.

Molly, an individual with OCD, shares how recognizing her OCD as neurodivergent was a lightbulb moment:

It helped me view my neurodivergent traits for what they are, rather than as something I was doing wrong. Obviously, I will always need treatment for the challenging parts of my diagnoses, but seeing my mental illness more as the way my brain works rather than something to fix is very helpful. It also opens the door for more ways to help me, such as when I'm feeling very overwhelmed. I can't just 'calm down'. My brain doesn't work that way.

Hannah shares this:

It means that I understand the world we have grown up in has been created for people who can work and live in a certain way. Understanding that I am divergent from the 'normal' way other people's executive function works gives me space to structure my world in a way where I can succeed.

Frank shares how viewing his bipolar experiences the same way as he views his Autistic experiences allows him to work with them rather than against them:

> Constantly fighting against my traits only makes them worse; trying to solve these 'problems' will only further them, but accepting my mood states and experiences lets me effectively live with them. Not to say that it is easy – it's not. But living a life free of self-harm, a life where I can better myself and improve lives around me, and one where I feel fulfilled would be impossible if I didn't see my bipolar traits as neurodivergent, and instead saw them as an illness, a diagnosis, a problem.

'I have more compassion and acceptance for myself'

Issac, an individual with schizophrenia, shares this:

> With self-compassion and the label of neurodivergent, rather than disordered, I've actually been able to develop much more care towards myself and the voices I hear – I can become softer and kinder, rather than feeling ashamed or angry at my experiences.

Lee, an individual with BPD, shares how viewing their BPD as neurodivergence would make a difference:

> The stigma that comes with having a personality disorder makes one feel like there's something deeply wrong with them. Even

the term 'personality disorder' makes it feel like my personality itself is broken. There's a lot of shame that comes with having BPD and I've personally isolated myself from others because I feel like I need to protect others from myself, when really I need to be showing myself love, compassion and understanding. If I viewed myself with the perspective that I am simply neurodivergent, perhaps I could feel less inner turmoil about having BPD.

AO, a mental health professional with BPD, shares how identifying as neurodivergent helps them:

It helps me to cope with BPD by viewing it as an adaptive function of my brain and nervous system instead of a problem within me. Viewing it as a function of my brain and nervous system helps me to identify ways to cope. For example, when having an episode of emotional dysregulation in response to objectively minor stimuli, I can tell myself that it makes sense that I'm having a hard time because, as someone with BPD, my amygdala is hyperactive. This helps me normalize my responses while also helping me to find ways to cope without having to work through a layer of heavy shame about my issues.

Ethie, who is Autistic with BPD and other specified dissociative disorder (OSDD), shares this:

Viewing my BPD and OSDD as facets of neurodivergence as opposed to a 'mental illness' or 'mental health disorder' would reduce the amount of shame I feel for having these diagnoses, both within myself and from others who are neurodivergent. It also diagnostically makes sense to me. There's no medication that 'cures' Autism, just as there's no medication that 'cures' BPD/NPD[1]/pretty much any other cluster B diagnosis. If I'm seen as neurodivergent when I say that my intense upset is caused by higher levels of empathy as a result of my Autism, why would the same label not apply when my intense upset is caused by higher levels of empathy *and* fear of abandonment from BPD? That doesn't make sense to me.

Dan Casey shares what neurodivergent means to them:

Finding ways to move through the world that genuinely work for me and make sense to me. Acknowledging who I am and how I operate from a place of acceptance, compassion, understanding and care, rather than as faults or deficiencies. Embracing my complete lack of interest in performing ableist, socially constructed, oppressive measures of 'productivity' and 'success' in order to prove my innate human value. Denouncing non-disabled dominance. So much less shame. So much more permission to do/be exactly who I am. Not living in constant conflict with my mechanisms and operating systems. So much less confusion and frustration over these aspects of myself that were *never* 'wrong' in the first place.

1   Narcissistic Personality Disorder.

'It challenges stigma and how mental health professionals as well as society view us'

Val shares how it would make a difference if mental health professionals saw schizophrenia as neurodivergent:

> I feel that if mental health professionals saw mental health conditions as neurodivergent rather than disorders or syndromes, then the stigma around these conditions would be lessened somewhat. If schizophrenia was seen as just another type of brain rather than something that is evil and wicked and to be cured, and instead just a part of someone's life and something that may need help being managed, and if the person with the condition was seen as a person that still requires enrichment and help, then it would improve the care of those with these stigmatized brains.

Zoe, who has major depressive disorder, shares how identifying as neurodivergent would make a difference to themselves and how mental health professionals understand them:

> It would be a step toward removing the shame around how my brain works, and as I've started to discover, shame and judgement is a big part of what makes my disorders dangerous to myself. If mental health professionals saw it as neurodivergent, they could work on making the world fit us, instead of training people to pretend to fit into the world. I could have someone talk to me about what makes my sadness so painful, instead of focusing on finding which pills will numb it enough to be normal. I wouldn't be treated as a problem with a character

flaw, but as a human with an equally valid understanding of the world.

Lizzie, a mental health professional with OCD, shares how there's a big difference between the narratives of neurodivergent vs disorder:

Neurodivergent feels more like a personal and important narrative, whereas disorder feels gross and pathologizing. I think if we went for the neurodivergent lens, it would decrease stigma and make everyone seem more human instead of a clinical diagnosis.

Sarah, a social work student with a personality disorder, shares what could happen if professionals viewed mental disorders through a neurodivergent lens:

I think the field would innovate faster and help more people more quickly and in more lasting, deeper ways. They would respect lived experience and value the insights of everyone, and therefore would have more chances of success due to having more perspectives informing their work. I think we would also be seeing more successful outcomes with a wider range of people because we would be working *with* rather than *against* people's needs and natural ways of being. As it stands, it really seems to me that professionals tend to try to force one way of being and one goal, even if they think they are being trauma-informed, person-centred.

Derrick Quevedo believes the perception of madness as differently functioning minds, rather than illnesses of the mind, can be used as a tool that can be used against dismantling carceral institutionalization, forced hospitalization and police intervention for those of us experiencing altered states, unusual realities and situations determined to be dangerous or uncomfortable by sanist standards.

Max, an individual with BPD and NPD, shares their thoughts on mental health professionals recognizing mental health conditions as neurodivergent:

> No one but I can decide if I am mentally ill, disordered or in need of healing, and I hate it when mental health professionals treat me as if my BPD is a tumour, because I don't see myself as ill. I think we need to reframe disorders as neurodivergences at least to stop the idea that we need treatment to 'heal completely' and to replace it with the goal of living our life in a way that suits us.

Hannah, an individual with BPD and bipolar, also agrees:

> Mental health professionals recognizing mental health conditions as neurodivergent would put less responsibility on the individual to conform to societal standards and more focus on accessibility and real accommodations.

Mason, an individual with OSDD, shares how they don't see the way their brain works as bad or wrong, but just different:

If mental health professionals saw it the same way, they could work with my brain instead of fighting it or trying to make me fit into the neurotypical box.

Alyss, who has a diagnosis of OCD, bipolar and BPD, believes there would be more compassion and maybe even more opportunity for truly accessible, patient-directed care if mental health conditions were viewed as neurodivergent. Alyss points out beautifully:

Less pathology leaves room for curiosity.

Drew, who is a part of a dissociative identity disorder (DID) system, believes recognizing DID as neurodivergent would create better treatment:

There would be more focus on our own needs and how to help us in a way that actually benefits us rather than trying to 'fix' us or make us as 'normal' as possible. We're already normal, just a different kind of normal, and we don't need to be changed or fixed; we just need support and understanding of who we are.

Ren, an Autistic ADHDer with OCD, believes recognizing more mental health conditions as neurodivergent would allow for kinder and more understanding approaches from professionals:

It would help lessen the opportunities for bias and judgement and stigmatizing by those within the field and thus could stop these professionals passing on these attitudes to their patients, and I believe it could allow more space for more holistic treatment and management plans for everyone, but particularly people with multiple diagnoses.

Jane, an individual with BPD, premenstrual dysphoric disorder (PMDD) and anxiety plus depression, believes recognizing mental health conditions as neurodivergent would move towards adapting and accessibility:

I don't think it has been helpful to expect my brain to change and no longer be anxious and obsessive; this has hindered my ability to move forward. I don't feel 'normal' in how I manage relationships; this hasn't changed in the past ten years, despite being in BPD 'remission'. I think professionals moving towards a neurodivergent space would support a more functional treatment and support plan for those living with these conditions - including me! I have learned more about adapting and accessibility for myself since working with my neurodivergent clients in art therapy.

I hope you can feel the impact that identifying as neurodivergent has had on individuals and how they view themselves, understand themselves and support themselves. I hope you can see how identifying as neurodivergent has helped individuals advocate for their differences and needs. I hope you can tell, by reading these stories, the difference that it makes identifying as neurodivergent over having a disorder.

Identifying as neurodivergent isn't just another label; it's also an identity, it's a reclamation, it's a song. When we call ourselves neurodivergent, we are reclaiming our differences that society calls abnormal, wrong or disordered. When we call ourselves neurodivergent, we are saying that while we may diverge from dominant societal norms, it doesn't mean our existence, our differences, our functioning are abnormal or wrong. When we call ourselves neurodivergent, we are challenging you to consider what 'normal' actually means and perhaps even realize that maybe our normal isn't your normal. When we call ourselves neurodivergent, we are rejecting the concept of disorders.

CHAPTER 7

Intersections of Gender, Sexuality, Race, Disability and Neurodiversity

I would like you to picture this: you're standing in the middle of a busy junction and you have traffic coming at you from all four directions; if you're lucky, you might experience a few near misses, and if you're extra lucky, someone may stop to help you, but either way, you're in the middle of an intersection and you're going to get hit. That is what it's like living at the intersection of different identities: you have traffic, in the form of marginalization and oppression, coming at you from all directions. As a white, queer and disabled neurodivergent, that's four identities, and one of those identities gives me a lot of privilege. If we want to keep going with my analogy, I might be standing in the middle of an intersection with four roads but one of those roads is empty of traffic, which means I've only got three roads that I need to worry about. While there is plenty of traffic coming at me from three directions, there's still one less direction, which affects my chances of getting hit by traffic. I'll experience several misses (fewer barriers), I might get hit by a car rather than a truck (less discrimination) and I'll probably get help a lot faster (access to support and resources). If someone holds multiple identities that are marginalized, they're standing at an intersection with traffic coming from all directions, which means there is more risk of suffering and harm. Put simply, I'm standing in the middle of a three-way junction and they're standing in the middle of a four-lane intersection during peak hour.

It's why Kimberlé Crenshaw developed the term 'intersectionality'. Kimberlé wanted to describe the unique combination of barriers experienced by women of colour,[1] and over time, it has become a framework for us to understand the unique dynamic of marginalization, oppression and privilege when you hold multiple identities. It is a lens for understanding how power and inequality intersect, entwine and impact each other.

While the concept was originally used to examine and understand the intersection of gender and race, intersectionality now includes multiple identities and communities, which is why we should absolutely apply it to neurodiversity, too. We need an understanding of intersectionality because understanding neurodiversity and supporting neurodivergent individuals would be incomplete if we don't understand all of someone. When someone is neurodivergent, they have different experiences to someone who is neurotypical, but if you add in gender, disability, race, culture and socioeconomic circumstances, the experiences are even more different, with many layers.

I am queer, neurodivergent and physically disabled, which means I experience oppression, barriers and discrimination, but

---

1   Kimberle Crenshaw, 'Demarginalizing the Intersection of Race and Sex: A Black Feminist Critique of Antidiscrimination Doctrine, Feminist Theory, and Antiracist Politics [1989]', in Feminist Legal Theory: Readings in Law and Gender, ed. Katherine Bartlett (New York, Routledge, 2019), 57–80. https://doi.org/10.4324/9780429500480-5

I'm also white, which means I also experience a lot of privilege. I cannot ignore or dismiss that privilege because it changes my experiences of being non-binary, neurodivergent and disabled. I'm able to unmask in public because people do not perceive me as dangerous, I'm less likely to have people call the police when I experience a meltdown and I'm also more likely to receive access to support and resources. As Tiffany Hammond, a Black Autistic parent and author of *A Day with No Words*, writes on her Instagram, 'I can't just hide certain stims because "it looks weird", I have to hide them because it looks weird, but also threatening and I am now unemployable and most often, a poor reflection on the whole of Black people.'[2]

Acknowledging intersectionality means recognizing that our identities impact our experiences; our experiences are different when we hold different identities. As a white Autistic, I'm far less likely to experience consequences if I'm stimming in public, while a Black Autistic is far more likely to experience consequences if stimming in public. Sure, we're both Autistic but our experiences are different and it's really important to acknowledge this, especially if you want to have any hope of understanding or supporting neurodivergent individuals.

Our identities are a package deal, and for many individuals with intersecting identities and lived experience, there is a whole other set of barriers, marginalization and discrimination. We need to recognize intersectionality when it comes to neurodiversity because we genuinely cannot dismantle one system without dismantling all the systems. Asiatu Lawoyin, who writes for NeuroClastic, shares the importance of dismantling all systems because as Asiatu writes, 'I am a culmination of my identities, which all shape my experience

2   Tiffany L. Hammond (@fidgets.and.fries), 'Autistic people, mask. Black people, code switch', Instagram, 3 May 2022. www.instagram.com/p/CdEaIiSv3oh

of this world and are interconnected with systemic oppression. I am AFAB/trans, which is erased by patriarchy. I am Black, which is erased by White Supremacy and racism. I am Autistic, which is erased by ableism.'[3] I mean, we simply cannot address and disrupt one form of oppression without addressing all forms of oppression, and we cannot support someone's identity without supporting all of their identities.

It isn't just us personally who need to recognize and understand intersectionality. We also need services and systems like the government, healthcare, workplaces and education to understand intersectionality and be intersectional.

And it needs to be reflected in policies, research, accommodations and solutions, because we need them to address the whole of the person, we need them to understand all of us, we need them to address all of us. As Morénike Giwa Onaiwu shares in an article on her blog:

> I – and people like me – can't splinter ourselves. There is no disabled me. There is no black me. There is no female me. There is no parent me. There is no Christian me. There is just...me. All of me. And I need for all of me – all these parts of me – to be addressed. I can't leave my leg out in the rain while the rest of my body comes indoors for shelter. Because if I do I am still going to be wet and miserable, even if much of my body is dry. That won't work for me.[4]

When you don't see yourself reflected in research, in policies, in stories, in media, in everyday environments, it reinforces the

---

3   Asiatu Lawoyin, 'The intersectionality of my erasure: Being AFAB, Black, & autistic', NeuroClastic, 2 March 2022. https://neuroclastic.com/the-intersectionality-of-my-erasure-being-afab-black-autistic
4   Morénike Onaiwu, 'All of me: How do I know where blackness ends and neurodivergence begins?' Who Needs Normalcy, blog post, 31 December 2018. www.whoneedsnormalcy.com/2015/12/all-of-me-how-do-i-know-where-blackness.html

message that you don't count, your needs don't matter, your experiences don't matter. It's an indication of society not seeing us, not valuing our existence. We need to consider and understand intersectionality when it comes to supporting neurodivergent individuals because no one wants to be half seen, no one wants to feel half accepted. Everyone deserves access to resources, support and services that meet all of their needs, and everyone deserves access to environments and spaces that are dedicated to dismantling all barriers, not just some barriers. If you aren't familiar with intersectionality, I hope the following discussions, stories and contributions can serve as a brief introduction where you can read people's experiences and insight into the unique dynamic of having multiple identities. I am immensely grateful that I have the honour of including the written pieces of Derrick Quevedo, Charli Clement, Nia Patterson and Dr Mari Cerda, who each exist at the intersection of multiple identities.

The intersection of race and neurodivergence

Neurodivergent refers to someone whose functioning diverges from dominant societal norms, and, as you now know, these dominant societal norms, standards and expectations are rooted in white supremacy culture. As Regina Ivy says, it is a culture 'that makes it a lot easier to succeed if you are white, straight, able-bodied, and neurotypical. Neurodivergent diverges from *this* standard. A standard that Black people are not capable of ever fully reaching.'[5] As Regina Ivy emphasizes, we must understand neurodivergence outside of a white context in order for neurodiversity and neurodivergence to be fully inclusive. We cannot dismantle ableism without dismantling

5   Regina Ivy, 'Black neurodivergent can't exist in white contexts', The UIS Observer, 1 March 2022. https://uisobserver.com/top-stories/2022/03/01/black-neurodivergent-cant-exist-in-white-contexts

racism, and for that, we need to talk about the intersections of race and neurodivergence. As a white person, I obviously cannot speak on this particular intersection, which is why I am honoured to introduce Dr Mari Cerda, Nia Patterson and Derrick Quevedo who will share their words and insights of living at the intersection of race and neurodivergence.

Neurodivergence and Race
By Dr Mari Cerda

In discussing the intersections of neurodiversity and race, it is imperative that I preface that, first, in no way should my perspective lead one to feel as though this conversation is a sort of Oppression Olympics, and, second, to simultaneously acknowledge the reality that the colour of one's skin can and often does serve as a protective factor for other less visible or invisible intersections. Race, and more specifically skin colour, is the one intersectional cord weaving through all of the other intersections that remains a primary point of contention. It is the often violently rejected truth that racism and ableism are two sides of the same philosophical coin, with the racism side face down out of reluctance to tackle.

You see, even at the intersections of neurodiversity and gender diversity, racism continues to rear its ugly head even among these marginalized groups. Black and Brown communities both with and without disabilities are far too familiar with this reality. In the US, we know that Black and Brown children are disciplined at disproportionate rates in comparison to their white peers. Black and Brown children are also misdiagnosed more often with disorders such as ODD (Oppositional Defiant Disorder), conduct disorder, and even intellectual disabilities due to a continued lack of understanding of how Autism and other neurodivergences manifest in non-white communities.

Neurodivergence does not provide an individual with immunity against racism or even colourism, and this is clearly evidenced through various advocacy movements and the perpetuation of racism in so-called designated safe spaces that continue to centre the white neurodivergent experience. Manifestations of neurodivergence in Black and Brown adults are often misunderstood and attributed to negative traits associated with race or colour. For example, a white woman with ADHD may exhibit impulsive behaviours such as talking over others, or interrupting, and those may be more willingly accepted as part of their neurodivergence, whereas Black and Brown women with ADHD are more likely to have those behaviours attributed to being an 'angry Black woman', or a 'hot-headed Latinx'. Even in 2SLGBTQIA[6] spaces deemed as 'safe', Black and Brown individuals report encountering hateful and racist rhetoric.

Even advocacy efforts are heavily driven and influenced by the impact on white disabled communities, despite the detrimental results of these efforts on their Black and Brown community members. For example, the anti-ABA movement is one of the rare moments in history where the protective factor of whiteness did not provide safety against abusive systems and practices that occur in this field. In this context, individuals who unknowingly benefitted and were somewhat protected across other systems due to their proximity to whiteness (such as speech and language pathology, occupational therapy, cognitive behavioural therapy, medical systems, educational systems, judiciary systems) were exposed to the racism and ableism in

6   Two-Spirit, Lesbian, Gay, Bisexual, Transgender, Queer, Intersex, Asexual/ Agender.

ABA therapy that Black and Brown communities have navigated for the last 300 years across all of the systems listed above.

Across these systems of medical and mental healthcare, education, religion and law enforcement, Black and Brown communities have consistently been wedged between surviving and thriving. Black disabled women are the most likely to be harmed or killed in our modern medical system, and yet these systems that harm are the same systems they must rely on to save their lives in other situations. We are all too familiar with the necessary paradox of navigating systems designed to oppress and harm us in order to receive access to aspects of those systems that also keep us alive.

Two other critical factors that should be considered when discussing race are the influence of geographic location and socioeconomic status. Black and Brown communities can't be viewed simply as a monolith due to socioeconomic status and geographic location contributing to one's access to awareness, education and understanding of disability and neurodivergence.

The experiences of Black communities on the East and West Coasts vary vastly and also in comparison to Black communities of the South. The experiences of Black communities in the UK and other countries also differ greatly from their US counterparts. Brown communities include Latinx, Indigenous, and other non-white groups with unique lived experiences around race and neurodiversity. When addressing neurodiversity across race and colour, it's necessary for dominant groups to understand the amount of diversity even across Black and Brown communities in order to refrain from using a tactic of 'wedging' or a sort of pitting of two non-dominant groups against each other due to their unique lived experiences around race and neurodivergence.

In order to ensure that we tackle head on both sides of the

coin of racism and ableism, our neurodivergent community has a responsibility to recognize and dismantle potential gatekeeping of advocacy among non-dominant groups as well as recognizing current advocacy efforts centring white experiences that inadvertently harm our Black and Brown community members.

Twice as Hard and Making Half as Much Sense
By Nia Patterson

There's something funny about me thinking that this Black boy I heard about in the news and I are on a first-name basis because we are both Black.

Sure, we are both running the rat race of being Black and neurodivergent in America. So, why wouldn't we be on a first-name basis?

We're both neurodivergent.

Both Black.

Both have a voracious love of music.

He, however, is more of a cat person than I am. I prefer dogs.

We both are in our 20s.

The only difference that matters is what keeps us worlds apart.

He is dead. I am living. I am alive.

And against the bad judgement of the police and the judicial system, I plan to stay that way.

His name is Elijah. Elijah McClain.

You may have heard of him. Elijah.

You may know his name and have marched under that title. You may have held signs emblazoned with his face and screamed his name in the face of police officers.

I just know him as another casualty of this war.

This is America in 2022. We are in a civil war.

But no one will call it that because Black people aren't seen as human in the same way that white people are.

In today's age, Black people are under attack by White America.

White Supremacy more specifically.

To be Black in America is to be unsafe. It is to be the least safe and the first to disappear. It is to worry if when you do disappear, or your death is published on social media, that you won't matter enough to be protested for.

I spend nights and days frozen in terror of how I could die at any moment in this war.

What's worse than a civil war of Black and White? It's that every layer of marginalization that you add to that racial disparity brings you steps closer to microaggressions, bullying, blatant racism, and even death.

You cannot escape your race; you wear it on your sleeve every day.

You can disguise your brain, however. You can hide and cover up your brain's eccentricities and unusual traits if you're lucky. If you're not so lucky, then you end up like Elijah or countless other dead Black folx.

Neurodivergence isn't just a diagnosis. For some, it is a death sentence. It's a toe tag in the morgue.

There are countless names that go on that list.

Whether they were diagnosed or not, they may have threatened a system built on cookie-cutter thoughts, neurotypical brains, and straight-edge ideas. That divergence from the norm led to a death that came much sooner.

I am not only scared to live my life some days in my skin,

dark brown skin, but even more so now that I have more clarity on my own neurodivergence as well.

Prior to June of 2022, I was very aware that I fit under the neurodivergent umbrella. I don't have a couple of diagnoses on that list but several that affect me. Some began in childhood and others developed in my teenage years or adulthood.

Sometimes it feels like I have collected different diagnoses as if they were baseball cards, although not intentionally.

Earlier this year my list of diagnoses was long and included ADHD, OCD, bipolar II disorder, cPTSD, PTSD, an eating disorder, among others.

One note is that despite showing traits for years, it wasn't until after I graduated college that I was diagnosed with ADHD.

It took me years of adulthood for someone, my therapist at the time, to look at me and point out that I possessed a number of traits characteristic of ADHD. She referred me to a psychiatrist who confirmed that suspicion within minutes.

I didn't know what that meant, though. I did some googling on my own and researched the words, 'adult ADD' and found details like forgetfulness, misplacing items, quick speech patterns, and other things that I felt sort of fit me. But I didn't realize that what I had stumbled upon in therapy had a much bigger impact than a line on my patient chart.

I was not put on meds specifically for my ADHD at the time. No one followed up to tell me what ADHD actually was, how it presented, how it affected me, or anything else that might have been helpful. My appointments just went on as if nothing had changed, so I figured it really hadn't and I slipped ADHD to a back-burner concern.

In the meantime, I spent my time repeatedly trying to define myself by society's norms (aka neurotypical principles).

Trying to keep up utterly exhausted me. Keeping up with the expectations of my job and trying to 'adult' drained me.

I didn't realisze that at the time I was very blatantly experiencing burnout.

Instead of explaining executive functioning, I was told I was just mildly depressed.

I continued to drag myself along, doing the very best that I could on any given day.

Sure, my brain was behind the driver's wheel but the car must have been built backward or something because things were twice as hard and made half as much sense.

The medical system consistently lets neurodivergent folx down.

The medical system lets Black folx down.

The medical system lets queer folx down.

The medical system lets fat folx down.

The medical system lets trans folx down.

The medical system is honestly shit most of the time. And on a good day, it lets most people who don't fit society's preferred norms down AND, often, it even lets them die.

On at least two occasions, I fully and completely surrendered to the burnout that was constantly nipping at my heels. The first was in college when I learned I had chronic depression and anxiety. I struggled tooth and nail through that semester accompanied by skipped classes and days of not eating.

The second time was in 2017, three years after I graduated college, when all of it (the burnout, depression, exhaustion and overworking) finally caught up to me and dragged me down.

The eating disorder I had engaged in for years had been simmering, but after throwing gasoline on it in high school and then again in college, by now it was a raging bonfire.

I couldn't manage my mental health on my own anymore.

That year I finally took the reins, admitting to myself and those around me that it was 'not okay' by far. I closed my business, left the place I was renting, took a leave of absence from work, and admitted myself into treatment for my eating disorder.

I spent from February until July in treatment working as hard as I could to get better. But it only mattered so much since the treatment facility wasn't made for my brain or my body. It wasn't made for a fat, Black, neurodivergent person like me, and so I made strides but didn't thrive or succeed how they wanted me to.

People thought I was letting them in when in reality they had never been further away from me. The reality of the wall I had put up was one of the loneliest experiences I have ever known.

It lasted until I was supposedly 'healed' and discharged from treatment by an insurance company that had never met or talked to me. It couldn't have been further from the truth. I was still sick.

I spent the next six months in a hole of burnout recovery. I lay in bed all day and watched back-to-back TV show episodes. I drove an hour and a half in each direction for human contact most days. I did my best to convince myself to eat my meals.

It took me those six months to recover enough from burnout to even consider taking on adult responsibilities again. Even so, at that time, had it been my choice, I would have stayed in bed and continued to heal the pain of the years of psychological torture that had been waged in my own head.

From racism to fatphobia to homophobia to the pain of trying to fit into a society not made for me was beyond tiring.

Nonetheless, when early 2018 came and my disability payments ran out, I was forced to re-enter the world. I jumped back into the world I had previously known of poorly treated and misdiagnosed mental illness.

Years later, I found myself in a new state, with a new job and my own apartment.

This time it was the summer of 2020, mid-pandemic and far from ideal stress levels. My brain was on stimulants now and I behaved like it. I was working hard, running my business, working a full-time job, producing a podcast, and more.

I was definitely not okay but I didn't know how to be anything else.

Life had never taught me a way to be anything other than the 'gifted, smart child' and so I maintained that role through every season of life.

I kept my chin as high as I could and still see where I was going. The idea of letting someone down or not being perfect was a downward spiral I didn't have time to dip my toes into.

Now, we step into 2021 at a point where my ADHD has become so intense that it's now a struggle to even keep track of tasks and work that needs to be done.

I can't seem to keep a single thought in my head for long enough to write it down.

The exhaustion and burnout once again are nearly traumatizing. I've started yet another round of trauma therapy work, and I'm mostly stable in my recovery from my eating disorder.

But still, something feels wrong. Like the feeling of the seam of socks lying across the tops of your toes – something you can live with but that also kind of feels like death.

That's where things were in my life at the time until one day I watched an ADHD TikTok that hit the nail on the head for me.

This one weird, quirky trait that I have is actually a symptom of ADHD. The lack of object permanence.

At my next therapy session, I bring up the video, and for the first time in all these years, we finally start to talk about what ADHD is. We talk about how it affects me in my day-to-day life. Why I can't remember anything anymore. My therapist breaks down why I feel so bored at my full-time job and how it's normal for people with ADHD to struggle with executive function – well, first, she explained what executive function actually was.

Finally, someone was taking the time to explain to the really smart, really talented, gifted, Black person what the diagnosis they've had for five years meant.

This time when I researched 'Adult ADHD', I had more understanding, and also a lot more resources like Instagram and TikTok. Those platforms explained things quickly and in ways I understood and could grasp.

Even then, it wasn't until the summer of 2022 that I finally became comfortable with having ADHD and also the fact that I no longer identify as a woman. I have learned so much more about who I am and how I function, how to motivate myself, and that I actually need rest and care even when I don't feel like it. It took a solid year of work to discover most of these things and also that time to learn how to implement the care needed to manage them.

This is just a snapshot of my life story. A brief stint in the world as my brain knows it and has dealt with it. But I want to take a moment to share some of what I have learned during my journey to where I am today and where I hope to end up.

Here are some ways you can show up for and support your neurodivergent friends:

- Don't ask too much of your neurodivergent friends. Ask for what you need and check in that what you're asking is reasonable. And furthermore, if they say they don't want to or can't handle it, then take that answer and accept it. Respect their boundaries and capabilities.

- Do invite your neurodivergent friends to events or to hang out, even if they may not have liked it in the past. It should always be up to that person to decide what they can and cannot handle, not you. And we'd love to be invited to the same things you're doing even if we may turn down the offer.

- Don't obsess over labels or whether someone 'fits the criteria' you have laid out in your head. If that person uses a label or refers to themselves a certain way, *believe them*. It's their life and their designation.

- Do give your friends space when they ask for it. If they're dealing with burnout, it may take days or weeks, and sometimes months, for them to recover. If they ask for space, give it to them. But that doesn't mean don't keep communication open. They may need an offer from you to send over a meal or a ride to therapy. Give your friends space but don't cut them off.

Something that is ever present for me as a neurodivergent person *and* a Black person is the impressive prevalence of microaggressions. If you don't know what microaggressions are, they are:

the everyday slights, indignities, put downs and insults that people of colour, women, LGBT populations or those who are marginalized experience in their day-to-day interactions with people.[7]

Microaggressions are harmful because even though they may seem harmless to most people, they do just as much damage as overt oppression to the recipient.

Most people rarely realize they're even engaging in micro-aggressions or that what they're saying can have a direct influence on someone else. And that is hard. Don't get me wrong.

But as a person with multiple identities, here's what you need to know about why it's so important to not engage in microaggressions as much as humanly possible.

• They're actually still an 'ism' – racism, sexism, ableism...

• Experiencing a microaggression can be just as violent (because yes, they are violent) as overt and conscious racism. It can shut a person down and scare them.

• It can be understandable that you might not know you used a microaggression since they are so much a part of regular conversation in some situations. But if someone points out that you used one or that they were negatively affected by what you said, then stop, reflect, apologize, and do better moving forward.

• You wouldn't want to hurt the people close to you, right? And racism and microaggressions do just that, so try to avoid them.

7   Derald Wing Sue, 'Microaggressions: More than just race', Psychology Today, 17 November 2010. www.psychologytoday.com/us/blog/microaggressions-in-everyday-life/201011/microaggressions-more-just-race

Lastly, I just wanted to give my Black neurodivergent babes a few affirmations that have landed for me. As someone who really struggles with affirmations, these actually feel affirming and truthful to me, and I hope that maybe you are able to take something away from one or two of these.

- Give yourself grace. You are allowed to make mistakes, mess up, and not do things how you thought you were going to originally.

- You're doing the best you can with the knowledge and resources you have been given.

- What if the way you exist and live as a human on this planet was perfect just the way it is? Sit with that.

- Your humanness is enough just as it is. There are no criteria you have to meet to be enough for the world.

It's Lonely

By Derrick Quevedo

Two things can be true: we are never alone; we can always feel lonely.

I have never felt whole in social spaces. Throughout my life, I have found community within my respective multiply marginalized identities but have always had to sacrifice the vulnerable, more susceptible parts of me that need protection when they have not felt welcome or safe with others. It was lonely being the Brown kid in white schools and a white town. Being Brown immediately othered me and made me a target of bullying but it was also lonely when you were bullied by the Brown kids, too. My diagnosis of bipolar and Autism happened well into my 30s, so I've spent the majority of my life unclear why I am who I am.

It's also lonely as you grow into your more authentic self and lose relationships with others who cannot, or will not, accept you, including your access needs and your liberation from oppressive systems. Being multiply marginalized, it can be challenging for others to understand how liberation for one identity is connected with liberation for another – like how race and decolonization connects with madness and neurodiversity – and having to explain many seemingly disparate ideas and making all of it seem very convoluted and incoherent.

It's also lonely in love.

It's lonely when Asian men are statistically among the most disadvantaged at online dating (along with Black women), and when you finally match with someone, they unmatch with you upon learning that you're bipolar, assuming that you are burdensome, a challenge, a handful and possibly even dangerous. It's even lonelier when you seek peer support and compassion in neurodivergent spaces and folks refuse to see conditions labelled mental illnesses as neurodivergent.

It's also lonely when the infantilization of Autistic folks is combined with the emasculation of Asian men. You're deemed immature because you have brightly coloured stim toys, and you're not manly enough because you're not white and tall with a thick beard and wraparound sunglasses, holding up a large fish you've just caught, I guess.

It's lonely to navigate and feel belonging in historically white, neurotypical subcultures – and it's heartbreaking when these subcultures revolve around your special interests. It's lonely trying to enjoy social situations where you can be passionate about your passions with others, when you're alienated by the prevalent racism, ableism or misogyny. It's also lonely because these subcultures are commonly small, intimate, tight-knit scenes and are susceptible to gatekeeping and exclusivity, whether or not it's intentional. Marginalized and resilient folks within these spaces are few and far between, and establishing connections and friendships is already difficult when it's challenging to socialize like a neurotypical. If you can't be with your fellow nerds and outcasts, who can you be with?

It's lonely when white-facilitated and/or white-majority neurodivergent spaces forget how race affects our neurodivergent experiences, or that racialized folks are not a monolith; our specific racial, ethnic and cultural identities create unique neurodivergent identities, challenges, microaggressions and access needs, and those experiences can be a challenge to both communicate and to comprehend.

It's lonely when cultural gatekeeping is a common experience among many racialized and immigrant folks in the so-called USA, and any difficulty with social cues is perceived as either being 'too Americanized' or 'too foreign' but never neurodivergent.

It's lonely to ruminate in isolation over your missteps at masking around allistic white people and the unspoken responsibility of defying negative racial stereotypes around them, because we don't want to encourage their hateful xenophobia by justifying their preconceptions of us. It's also lonely when you've been alone in your home for weeks because you're still recuperating from the constant masking and code switching and juggling of multiple sets of neurotypical behaviours, from the white American co-workers to the white American punks to the Pilipino Americans to the Asian Americans to the homeland Pilipinos who look down on you for being American.

It's lonely when you come from a racialized immigrant

community that proudly defines itself on the importance of communal values, and yet the community stigmatizes you and does not respect your access needs. It's lonely when they conflate community with conformity, and the idea of a strong community is defined by everybody assimilating to a status quo created for and by sane, non-disabled neurotypicals.

It's lonely when the closest expressions of madness and neurodivergence in your native tongue are derogatory. It's lonely to be on the path towards decolonization when those derogatory terms are Indigenous and not borrowed language from the non-disabled, sane, ableist, neurotypical white supremacy of your colonizer.

It's lonely when you don't want to be continually ostracized for preferring less flavoured food or the same food ('Filipinos whose favourite dish is adobo are so basic!', 'What's the matter, Derrick, can't you handle the spiciness/sourness/bitterness? Aren't you a "real" Filipino?') It's lonely to be ostracized for eating anything overwhelmingly flavourful with a spoonful of rice to balance out the intensity, or for not allowing others to add sauces on my plate for me.

It's lonely when my hypomania and meltdowns are perceived as the privileged temper tantrums of a 'PilAm' ('Pilipino American', a title often used derogatorily back in the Philippines), and it's lonely to know that I would be shunned and shamed as the 'village crazy' if I was back home.

It's lonely to live with the fear of experiencing hypomania and Autistic meltdowns knowing that mad and neurodiversity awareness within the PilAm community is virtually non-existent. The fear of interactions with the police during such states is very real for racialized folks, including PilAms. After police were involved with Angelo Quinto's death (called by his family during a 'mental health crisis') in December 2020, our community wasn't particularly inspired to learn how to create safe, self-sufficient community support systems for those experiencing altered and extreme states, which didn't rely on the state to intervene. In community discussions and grief spaces, people like me were talked about and talked over. Whenever I expressed the idea that communities keep themselves safe, I was asked if I went to therapy. What I was really asked was if I was taking personal responsibility for not going crazy in the first place and disturbing the status quo with my hypomania and Autistic meltdowns, because my safety isn't the community's obligation. I felt beyond alone in those moments. I felt even more alone when white bipolar comrades shared anecdotes of receiving overwhelming support during their mania in public spaces such as airports.

The allistic folks who 'encourage' me to keep searching for 'my community' don't feel the exhaustion, anxiety, harm and heartache from the constant change, unfamiliarity and microaggressions I experience. They don't have to count spoons and ration energy. They don't feel the constant self-gaslighting and internalized ableism of wondering if I am, in fact, 'too sensitive' or 'overreacting' and need to 'suck it up' and 'toughen up' because the 'perfect' community and the 'ideal' friend and 'ideal' romantic partner don't exist. It's lonely when your final, ruminating thought before bed is consistently 'Am I the problem?'

It's lonely when you accept more and more each day that this loneliness just might follow you for the rest of your life.

I am so grateful for Dr Mari Cerda, Nia Patterson and Derrick Quevedo and their contributions to this chapter. I approached these three individuals because I have learned so much from them by following them on social media and listening to their lived experience. I do want to express that this chapter and their contributions are not the end of understanding the intersection of race and neurodivergence. It is merely the beginning and we have so much more listening and learning to do. In saying that, I would like to share the names of a few other individuals who speak on the inter-section of race and neurodivergence: Tiffany Hammond (@fidgets.and.fries), Sandra Coral (@nd.narratives), TJ (@nigh.functioning.autism), Ryse T (@teachingwithmxt), Sandhya Menon (@onward-sandupwardspsych), V. Tisi (@speechologist), Candice Alaska (@understandingbpd) and Jules Edwards (@autistictyping). Follow them, listen to their lived experience, read their work, prioritize their voices and, most importantly, compensate and pay the individuals whose work you are learning from.

The intersection of gender, sexuality and neurodivergence

When it comes to gender, society has created expectations and norms that are forced upon us. It's similar to how society has cre-ated neuronormative expectations and norms that are forced upon us and to which we are expected to conform. I don't think gender and neurodivergence are so different, after all. I mean, both trans and neurodivergent individuals both diverge and refuse to conform to heteronormativity, cisnormativity and neuronormativity, and both trans and neurodivergent individuals are subject to being pathol-ogized as well as viewed as abnormal. As Eric Garcia says in their book *We're Not Broken: Changing the Autism Conversation*, 'the desire to eliminate the traits that make autistic people unique is rooted in the same impulse to suppress people from affirming their gender identity or sexuality'.[8] This same idea can be applied to all neurodivergent individuals. It comes down to society othering any differences, whether it's gender, sexuality, bodies or even our minds.

8   Eric Garcia, *We're Not Broken: Changing the Autism Conversation* (New York: Harvest Publications, 2021).

I'm Autistic and I am trans non-binary. I know I'm not a woman, but I also don't feel any urge to identify as a man either. In fact, I actually don't really relate to the concept of gender at all, and I believe being Autistic is a big part of why that is. In the same way I don't 'get' social norms, I don't 'get' gender. Lydia X. Z. Brown has previously discussed the intersection of Autistic and trans experiences with a similar sentiment: '[B]eing autistic doesn't *cause* my gender identity, but it is inextricably related to how I understand and experience gender.'[9] I feel like this is the case for many neurodivergent individuals, especially Autistic individuals. As we are often in a position to question norms, because we automatically diverge, we are often more likely, as well as more willing, to question gender and sexuality norms and embrace our queerness. I had the opportunity to share the experiences of a couple of neurodivergent individuals who are also trans or non-binary on how their neurodivergence impacts their relationship with gender. Laila, a non-binary neurodivergent individual, shares that being neurodivergent is what allowed them to question their gender in the first place:

Social rules have always bothered me, since I was a child and I always tried to go 'against the current' in several matters. I believe that being Autistic and ADHD was what made me question everything that is defined as 'right' and 'wrong' in society and also disagree with there being only one correct way to be.

On a similar note, Kai, a trans and non-binary individual, shares

---

9   Lydia Brown, 'Gendervague: At the intersection of autistic and trans experiences (repost),' Autistic Hoya, 16 May 2020. www.autistichoya.com/2020/05/gendervague-at-intersection-of-autistic.html

another experience on how much their neurodivergence impacts their understanding of gender:

> My neurodivergence and gender are so intrinsically intertwined in my understanding of my own past experiences, because they were both ways that I was fundamentally different and spent a long time without a name for. The intersection of my Autistic experience of struggling with social rules and social constructs and my experience as a trans person who wasn't able to fit into rigid expectations around girlhood and womanhood are so deeply tied together that it's hard to see where one ends and the other begins. Whether it's just timing or similarly intertwined, I've also found that I've gotten more comfortable allowing every part of my identity to exist at the same time. Whether that's my neurodivergence or trans experience or disability experience. They are all just a part of how I naturally experience the world, and the more I let myself have the space for one of them the more space I make for all of them.

As you can see, neurodivergence and gender are very much entwined for many individuals, which is why we need to recognize and understand the intersection of gender and neurodivergence. When I asked TS, a trans and Autistic individual to share how being neurodivergent impacts their relationship with gender, they said that it's hard for them to explain their gender or lack thereof to others:

> I don't fit into the script of being trans (born in the wrong body, always felt this way) and I don't know how to make my own explanation because it's an inside thing that I just know. It's not

> something I feel is explainable at least to someone who is not
> also of trans experience.

When we continue to create narrow boxes, narrow definitions and scripts that only follow a certain narrative, we end up excluding different experiences. When we don't recognize intersectionality or work to understand the intersection of different identities, we end up excluding individuals, which is what you'll find in the following personal example by TS who shares how being trans has made it harder to find mental health support because of the intersection of his identities:

> It's been really hard for me to find a therapist because I want one who is able to work with me as both an Autistic person and a trans person and I can barely find one who is experienced with either. This has made it very difficult to get help for my actual primary problem/the reason I need therapy which isn't either of those! It's anxiety! It has made my anxiety worse because it's been so hard to find treatment.

Providers who are neurodiversity affirming and understand neurodivergence are rare; providers who are neurodiversity affirming as well as LGBTQIA+ affirming are even more rare. If you're looking for a provider who is all of those things as well as anti-racist, you'll probably be looking for a while. As a result, it means neurodivergent individuals, queer individuals and people of colour can end up being harmed more by providers than they are helped. When it comes to seeking support from any provider, we need them to have an understanding of all our identities; we need providers to be intersectional.

It's also important for mental health providers and professionals to be aware of the intersection of gender and neurodivergence so we don't continue reinforcing gender stereotypes, standards, expectations or roles. Katie, a genderfluid, neurodivergent individual, in explaining how their neurodivergence impacts their relationship with gender, points out that 'a lot of gender roles come directly from cultural norms and tradition, and I've always seen tradition as something we should question and challenge, especially when it's just tradition for tradition's sake', which is similar to what A, a trans Autistic individual feels when it comes to understanding neurodivergence and gender:

> From a young age, gender rigidity and rules did not sit well with me. The idea that we are biologically determined to have to follow all of these socially constructed rules that are supposed to impact our personalities and how we engage in the world/ with others still does not sit well with me as an adult.

A also points out that many of the expectations and rules that are forced upon women often go against our neurodivergent needs and differences: 'it would bother me if I had to wear frilly, sequinny textures, and to force myself to do that because of some unfair and abstract rule'. They go on to say, 'the less I mask my Autistic self, the more colourful my gender comes through. The less I mask my vibrant gender, the more I allow myself to express my inner Autistic process outwardly. It's all intertwined.'

We need to recognize that neurodivergent individuals often hold multiple identities; we need to see all of the individual, not just one part of the individual. If we want to support and respect individuals, we need to respect the whole person. Katie shares some ways that people can show up for and support LGBTQIA+ and neurodivergent individuals: 'We need way more research into neurodivergence and how it intersects with gender and sexual diversity because the overlap is staggering.' While research into the intersection of gender and Autism is definitely increasing, we still need research that focuses on supporting our well-being, neurodivergence and gender identity. Katie also recommends that we need way more neurodivergent and queer people who can be visible in all aspects of life because, as Katie shares:

Growing up, I saw nobody like me and it really affected me. I felt like an alien, and it wasn't even on my radar that I could be gay or trans or neurodivergent at all! I tried fruitlessly for so long to be 'normal', doing countless hours of CBT and being overmedicated for so many misdiagnoses, trying to date men and wondering why I was so unhappy. The simple answer was that the neurotypical straight girl life just wasn't who I am, despite everything telling me it was. The media I consumed, the curriculum taught at my school, the therapy I was receiving, the culture I was brought up in - everything told me continually that I was incorrect and that I needed to change and be better.

This is why representation is so important, and it's also why representation needs to be intersectional. Individuals deserve to see themselves within media, within stories, within art, within research, because when you do see yourself, it makes you feel that who you are is okay and it makes you feel as though you're not alone. Plus, when you have accurate representation, it can also transform public opinion and get rid of stereotypes.

There's another way that people can show up for and support

LGBTQIA+ and neurodivergent individuals, and it comes down to presuming competence, respecting our autonomy and treating us as the experts of our own identities and experiences. It's a common experience for neurodivergent individuals to be viewed as lacking awareness, lacking insight or being unable to understand or make decisions. It's just one way that neurodivergent individuals are infantilized – where our autonomy is taken away. This impacts neurodivergent individuals when it comes to our gender and sexuality because there can be the assumption that we don't know any better, which is so far from the truth. TS reminds us that we must let neurodivergent individuals transition if they choose:

> Don't assume that just because someone is neurodivergent, it means that they can't make decisions about transitioning. We may not be able to answer all of your questions or perfectly explain our feelings – that doesn't mean we're making things up or wrong about ourselves. Treat us as the experts in our own lives.

Similarly, A wants everyone to remember to believe in us and affirm our knowledge of our own experiences:

> We know best who we are, we are the experts on our internal world. There is no one way to look Autistic/neurodivergent or LGBTQIA+. Please do not assume because we are neurodivergent that we can't know we are trans/non-binary, etc. Be an ally and disrupt the spreading of false/hateful messaging including anything that invalidates our difficulties, strengths and right to claim our identity. If you work in a field that is asked to gatekeep access to gender-affirming care, work actively against this.

> Use the language we model for you about our identities and when we ask you to use it for us.

Just because we are neurodivergent, it doesn't mean we don't know our gender or sexuality any less than someone who isn't neurodivergent.

I want to mention one other way that we can support LGBTQIA+ and neurodivergent individuals, and that's by ensuring community spaces and events that allow room for both identities, both forms of lived experiences. I cannot begin to describe the importance of community; when you're with community, you can be your authentic selves and you feel seen, safe and as though you belong. Community should be where all the parts of you are welcome and where your differences and needs are both respected and accommodated. Unfortunately, in many community spaces and community events, this isn't the case at all, which ends up excluding individuals who live on the intersection of these two identities. Kai, a trans and neurodivergent individual, shares a similar sentiment that a lot of queer spaces don't accommodate neurodivergent individuals:

> So much of queer culture and spaces are really exclusionary for folks with different brains because of the focus a lot of spaces have on being loud or drinking. Hannah Gadsby talks about this in a way that really resonates for me.

As a queer individual, I've always loved queer events but I struggle to attend them because they don't accommodate my neurodivergence. I would love to see queer venues and events where there are quiet spaces to take sensory breaks and where the focus isn't on drinking. In fact, I would love to see queer events where I, a queer and neurodivergent individual, feel represented – not just my queer identity but my neurodivergent identity, too. Give me a pride event with sensory accommodations or a pride event that doesn't revolve around alcohol. I want to see a drag queen night with sign-language interpreters. I want to see a drag queen stimming or wearing noise-cancelling headphones, please.

The intersection of disability and neurodivergence

When it comes to disability and neurodivergence, the intersection is huge because for many individuals, neurodivergence is a disability and for many individuals, we have co-occurring disabilities. I'm one of those individuals; I'm an Autistic ADHDer with bipolar and I'm also physically disabled with Ehlers–Danlos syndrome (EDS) and rheumatoid arthritis. I experience a lot of barriers when it comes to seeking support for my physical disabilities, especially when it comes to things like setting up appointments, filling in forms and even managing a number of specialists. There are many aspects that present challenges and barriers for me, such as making phone calls, travelling to appointments and following up on tests and exams. I even struggle with remembering medication and remembering to use my mobility aids.

My differences with interoception mean I find it a lot harder to be aware of what's going on for me physically, and, more often than not, my ADHD means I struggle to recall timelines, past injuries and past symptoms when communicating with specialists and doctors. I'm pretty certain some doctors have actually taken my pain or symptoms less seriously because I've been so vague in describing certain symptoms or I couldn't remember how long a flare-up has been occurring for. I've also had my pain and physical symptoms dismissed because of the stigma held by medical professionals against BPD, another of my neurodivergences. I've often been labelled as manipulative, cheating the system and even attention seeking because medical professionals have seen my BPD diagnosis on my medical chart.

Sarah, a neurodivergent individual with ADHD as well as EDS, who has a similar experience to mine, shares the ways that being disabled intersects with being neurodivergent:

EDS is a rare disease with many symptoms and no medical field responsible for it. Therefore, the level of self-management is high and there are between 10 and 15 different medical fields to attend to. With every medical appointment comes another 1-3 referrals to another specialist, to a university clinic, to a specialized therapist and that times 10-15. With my ADHD, I am completely overwhelmed and blocked, but also everything takes a long time as I often confuse appointments or forget them. The struggle is real with EDS, but my ADHD makes it even harder.

This is why we need to recognize the intersections of disability and neurodivergence – because supporting an individual and their disability requires supporting an individual and their neurodivergence. If we don't recognize someone's neurodivergence when supporting someone and their disability, we are merely creating more barriers, and, believe me, there are so many barriers in accessing healthcare whether you're neurodivergent or not. If you are neurodivergent, there are even more barriers. I would like to introduce neurodivergent and disabled advocate and author, Charli Clement.

The Connections Between Disabled and Neurodivergent

By Charli Clement

Disability and neurodivergence are inherently connected for me. I can't untangle them as separate entities. This isn't related to whether my being Autistic, ADHD and dyspraxic are 'positives' or 'negatives' to me – disabled and disability are neutral terms and don't mean I am putting myself down or ignoring all the ways my neurodivergent brain is wonderful.

There is this assumption that disability must be bad – we see it in the endless times non-disabled people try to make us change our language to something else. 'You're differently abled!' or 'You have special abilities' and endless other attempts all feed this same idea. I am constantly told that I can't be disabled because of the work I do or because that would be insulting myself. To me, just as my asexual identity is neutral, so is being disabled.

When it comes to the social model that much of the disabled community ascribes to, 'disabled' relates to the way that society disables us through the barriers it puts up, whether these be physical, social or sensory, for example (these are not the only categories).

I would, to an extent, still be disabled without just the societal barriers due to the nature of some of the ways my neurodivergence impacts me and the differences I experience compared to others. I would still struggle to remember to eat and drink, to look after myself, and this would be on top of my chronic pain and fatigue that I experience as part of my chronic illnesses that are co-occurring with my neurodivergences. However, this depends on how you look at the social model – as it can be argued the social model does allow for these difficulties too, with the idea that society would put in more support for these.

The human rights model of disability is subtly different, focusing on the person themselves in any and all decisions made about them, and placing the nature of disability within society. The final part there shows its similar nature to the social model, while placing more emphasis on the needs of the individual. Ultimately, within both of these models that I would ascribe to, the society that I live in and the nature of how we are naturally intertwined into a capitalist, ableist system mean that I am disabled.

I have a different relationship to my chronic illnesses than I do my Autism, ADHD and dyspraxia, in that the former I would get rid of in a heartbeat, and the latter I cannot imagine my world or self without – because I'll never know what that looks like. But, even with this separation, they are not separate when it comes to them both being disabilities. It is not the nature of my feelings about them that defines disability.

Society loves the superpower narrative when it comes to neurodivergent people, because it makes them so much more comfortable with it; often, it is used as a reason why we are employable and why the workforce should be employing more of us. My employability shouldn't be based on this – nor does this recognize the support we need.

And for me, a lot of the traits I have which people speak of as 'positive' and as superpowers are as equally neutral to me as my disabled identity. Hyperfocus can be great sometimes when it makes me work faster or when I can get really good at something quickly. But what about when my hyperfocus lands on TikTok for hours on end when I have a deadline, or when I end up not eating, drinking or going to the toilet for a whole day without even noticing?

Similarly, my sense of justice is a key to the work I do in advocacy; it means I have a drive incomparable to many and will go to the ends of the earth for the people I work with. But that means I spend most of my time so wrapped up in it that I can't think about anything except injustice and ableism and the elements of the world I hate so much. It is almost dizzying, stopping me from continuing to move forward.

My ability to remember lots of intricate details is useful in work capacities, but means I end up easily hyperfocused on my trauma because I remember the exact dates everything happened; I wish desperately sometimes that I could forget. And so it is all relative. My traits can be useful – but often only in the capitalistic sense. More often than not, they are significantly disabling and interrupt my days and intertwine with my trauma. It means I don't agree with the superpower narrative – but even if you do, there's nothing to say you can't call it a superpower and still be disabled, because these aren't opposites.

You don't have to believe you are disabled as a neurodivergent person – that is totally your right. But it is wrong to then ascribe this to every neurodivergent person, because neurodivergences *are* disabilities. On a purely practical level, we need them to be recognized as disabilities in order to get the support that society only makes available under technicalities and specific wordings or diagnoses.

Ignoring neurodivergence as being disabilities adds to stigma and means people can't access what they need – whether that is because society won't let them, or because they won't let themselves – and it is hard enough to access it as it is. Internalized ableism means that if these ideas are compounded, someone is likely to make themselves struggle.

It also leaves behind those who have higher support needs across different parts of their neurodivergence. I have varying support needs in different aspects of my own neurodivergence, but in the areas in which I have lower support needs, those are the ones society wants to capitalize on to pretend that neurodivergence isn't disabling and to ignore those who have higher support needs than me.

I find liberation in being disabled. I find so much beauty and identity and love within it.

Because it gives me a community of people who understand me, something I didn't have growing up, having no idea who I was or why I was different.

Because it means I am resisting the society we live in regardless of the way they want to mould me into something I am not and never have been.

Because it means I have an accurate descriptor that I feel comfortable and confident using.

Disability Justice and the movement towards it includes neurodivergent people. We are striving for something that empowers and liberates neurodivergent people with all of their different support needs, their intersecting identities, and that unroots the ableism that is so deeply embedded within society. Recognizing that is something so critical, that some of the narratives capitalism places on us and perpetuates doesn't support.

There's a lot of important advice stemming from lived experience here. We need to recognize the intersections of various identities because this often means we have different experiences, needs, barriers and more that we have to consider when understanding and supporting neurodivergent individuals. If we want to move towards a neurodiversity-affirming society, we need to make sure we are considering how other identities and experiences intersect with neurodivergence because the differences are huge. ChrisTiana ObeySumner, in an article titled 'Black autistics exist: an argument for intersectional disability justice', originally posted on South Seattle Emerald, shares why it's so important to consider intersectionality: 'When someone like me walks into the room, I don't have the opportunity to negotiate with others which of my identities they intend to hyperfocus on or criticize. I am a package deal.'[10] We need to consider the intersectionality of all identities because we are fighting for inclusion and acceptance for every single individual – for all our different ways of existing in this world. While I've been able to provide just a small snapshot of these intersections within this chapter, there is so much more learning needed, and it's up to each of you to continue listening to neurodivergent individuals who live at the intersection of these identities. I've tried to make your journey easier by recommending some books.

○ ○ ○

BOOKS TO READ ⬇

- *Gender Identity, Sexuality and Autism: Voices from Across the Spectrum* by Eva A. Medes and Meredith R. Maroney (Jessica Kingsley Publishers, 2019)

- *The Autistic Trans Guide to Life* by Yenn Purkis and Wenn Lawson (Jessica Kingsley Publishers, 2021)

- *All the Weight of Our Dreams: On Living with Racialized Autism* by Lydia X. Z. Brown, E. Ashkenazy and Morénike Giwa Onaiwu (DragonBee Press, 2017)

---

10 ChrisTiana ObeySumner, 'Black autistics exist: An argument for intersectional disability justice,' South Seattle Emerald, 6 December 2018. https://southseattleemerald.com/2018/12/05/intersectionality-what-it-means-to-be-autistic-femme-and-black

- *Disability Visibility: First-Person Stories from the Twenty-First Century* edited by Alice Wong (Vintage Books, 2020)

- *All Boys Aren't Blue* by George M. Johnson (Penguin, 2021)

- *Supporting Trans People of Colour: How to Make Your Practice Inclusive* by Sabah Choudrey (Jessica Kingsley Publishers, 2022)

- *So You Want to Talk About Race* by Ijeoma Oluo (Seal Press, 2018)

- *Me and White Supremacy: Combat Racism, Change the World, and Become a Good Ancestor* by Layla F. Saad (Sourcebooks, 2020)

CHAPTER 8

Neuronormativity: Challenging the Concept of Normal

As you now know, neurodivergent refers to any individual who has a mind or brain that diverges from dominant societal standards and norms. If your functioning and your ways of thinking, behaving, feeling, processing, communicating, learning, sensing and more fall outside what society deems 'normal', you are neurodivergent. What society deems normal, though, is actually the dominant norms, standards and expectations of Western society. We call it neuronormativity – a set of standards, expectations and norms that centre a particular way of thinking, feeling, functioning, behaving and communicating. See, normal has never been about what is actually normal; normal has always been about framing certain traits and certain ways of functioning as superior. It's what society has centred, the same way society has centred white people, able-bodied people, straight people and cisgendered people. As Dr Bex Canner (they/them) has stated in a blog post on LinkedIn, 'just like heteronormativity, a system in which queer people are pressured to perform like cisgender straight people, neuronormativity insists that [neurodivergent] people learn to perform like neurotypical people'.[1] The problem with neuronormativity is that it is seen as the one right way to be, and any deviation or divergence is labelled as abnormal and disordered.

I was diagnosed with bipolar because I experience extreme shifts in emotional and energy states. I was diagnosed with ADHD because how I think and pay attention is non-linear and inconsistent. I was diagnosed with BPD because how I experience emotions and relationships is different and often based on fear and insecurities. I was diagnosed with Autism because how I communicate, process information and experience the world is utterly different. There are so many parts of me that are seen as a disorder, as abnormal or wrong, but what if I could just be seen as different or maybe just diverging from how society expects me to be and function?

That's why we've got the term 'neurodivergent' because unlike the term 'disorder', which says we are broken and abnormal, neurodivergent doesn't imply we're broken for failing to live up to this societal construct of normal. Instead, we acknowledge we merely diverge from these standards, norms and expectations, and our differences, our needs and our challenges do not make us broken or abnormal. Imagine if there were people who could only experience the greens and blues of the colour spectrum and any deviation – anyone who experienced the reds and oranges – was labelled as abnormal or unwell. We would be pathologizing these individuals for seeing different colours, and all our focus would be on fixing them instead acknowledging the wonder in seeing different colours. Just as all the colours are a part of the colour spectrum, all the ways of existing and functioning in this world are a part of neurodiversity.

1   Dr Bex Canner, '"Neuronormativity" and gender performance', LinkedIn, 17 March 2022. www.linkedin.com/pulse/neuronormativity-gender-performance-bex-canner-they-them-

There are infinite ways to function, feel, think, behave, communicate, learn and exist as a human being – and, by golly, we need to make room for these differences. It's not going to be easy or even straightforward, but I hope we can start by challenging what we consider 'normal' by figuring out what these dominant societal norms are. If we're going to unpack these norms, we'll also need to consider where these norms, expectations and standards have come from and why.

Executive functioning

Executive functioning skills are a set of various mental skills or cognitive functioning skills. You might be familiar with some of them – such as planning, organizing and focusing on a task. In contrast, 'executive dysfunction' is a term to describe when individuals struggle with these particular skills, which leads to difficulty in completing tasks, managing time, regulating emotions, multitasking and remembering details or steps. It's a common experience for neurodivergent individuals, from Autistic individuals and ADHDers to individuals living with depression, PTSD and more. While it is true that neurodivergent individuals struggle with executive functioning skills, I would also argue that even neurotypical individuals struggle to maintain executive functioning skills every single day, which brings me to my main point: executive functioning skills are another set of neuronormative norms that don't account for our vast differences in functioning and existing. What if executive functioning is yet another neuronormative standard that we, as neurotypical and neurodivergent individuals alike, are expected to meet?

I read this great analogy once and wanted to share it in my own words. Executive functioning skills sound similar to the skills required to be a manager, a CEO or an executive. You need to be able to remember details, you need to be able to plan and organize activities in a straightforward and linear fashion, you need to be able to pay attention for an extended amount of time, you need to be able multitask and you need to be able to remain calm in different situations. Cool analogy, right? While those are great skills for a manager or an executive, we need to remember that not everyone is or even wants to be a manager or an executive, because we all have different strengths, skills and roles to play within society. If we can't all be executives and managers, why are these skills framed as the only way to function? If we can acknowledge that everyone has different strengths and skills in life, why are executive functioning skills any different?

I don't believe we should dismiss executive functioning skills as important skills, but I do believe we shouldn't frame them as the only skills to have. We need to appreciate the variety of skills. What if executive functioning skills aren't actually skills every single person must have but, instead, just a set of rules that dictate how we should function, where everyone has to follow these rules? We neurodivergent folks love to break and disrupt rules, and I feel like these particular rules are no exception. I want to challenge the idea that neurodivergent individuals have deficits where we lack these skills. I would like actually to propose that we are simply not meeting society's expectations around functioning, so let's see what it looks like if we reframe these skills as rules:

- You must be able to shift your attention from task to task immediately.

- You must be able to sustain your focus on a task for an extended period of time.

- You must be able to complete steps in a linear fashion.

- You must be able to provide the same amount of effort for all tasks.

- You must find all tasks equally motivating regardless of your values or interests.

- You must be able to remember all the steps of a task without any assistance.

- You must be able to remember details, no matter how long it's been, without any assistance.

- You must be able to start a task on demand.

- You must have the same priorities as everyone else when it comes to completing a task.

- You must be able to structure and organize things that make sense to everyone.

- You must be able to estimate how long a task will take with no information whatsoever.

- You must have the same definition of success as everyone else.

- You must be able to hide or suppress your emotions regardless of the situation.

Well, when you frame executive functioning skills as a set of rules, it sounds a bit ridiculous and unfair, right? I mean, how on earth can we all be expected to follow these rules all the time, especially when every individual is so different. Put simply, we can't and shouldn't all be expected to function or work a certain way; we're not all computers with the same operating system and programming. Personally, I don't want to be an executive when it comes to how I function. I would like to be able to get lost in my work without any external pressure to switch task. I would like to be able to respect my non-linear focusing as well as take breaks from focusing. I would like to complete the steps in a task that make sense to me. I would like to provide effort according to what I can provide at the time, without shame.

If executive functioning skills are a set of rules, why do these rules exist and where did they come from? We often have rules to achieve a goal, a purpose or a desired result. In a wonderful podcast called Disorderland by Jesse from Sluggish and Dr Ayesha Khan from Woke Scientist, Marta Rose says it best: executive functioning is 'a set of capitalist values masquerading as skills'.[2] We have these rules on how to function to meet the goals of capitalism and productivity because that is what Western society values:

- You must be a productive member of society in order to deserve life.

- Your worth or value is determined by your ability to work.

- It prioritizes profit and productivity over people's well-being and happiness.

- You must be independent and reliant only on yourself.

2   Dr Ayesha Khan and Jesse Meadows, 'Disorderland: Eo2: Kill the executive in your head w/ Marta Rose', Apple Podcasts, 18 April 2022. https://podcasts.apple.com/au/podcast/eo2-kill-the-executive-in-your-head-w-marta-rose/id1616515030?i=1000557945026

- We must be constantly producing or accomplishing.

It's also important to acknowledge that capitalism is a product of white supremacy and merely upholds the values of white supremacy, which is why I believe we need to consider how white supremacy relates to those pesky executive functioning rules that we call skills.

In this section, the following 13 White Supremacy Culture characteristics, and the non-verbatim definitions are taken from Tema Okun and Kenneth Jones's 2001 *Dismantling Racism Workbook*; a list of these characteristics can also be found on www. WhiteSupremacyCulture.info.[3]

Only One Right Way
One Right Way is the belief that there is only one right way to do things where individuals are expected to also follow the one right way and if they do not, they are the individuals who are wrong. I feel this is one of the most clear-cut explanations as to why these rules around executive functioning exist. We have determined one right way of doing things which has resulted in a set of executive functioning skills that are the right skills to possess. One Right Way has created a set of rules, expectations and standards that has led to a narrative of normal and abnormal. You must be able to shift your attention from task to task and be able to sustain your focus on a task for an extended period of time because this is the right way to pay attention. You must be able to complete steps in order because doing anything out of order isn't the right way.

3   Tema Okun, 'White Supremacy culture characteristics', White Supremacy Culture. Accessed 28 October 2022 at www.whitesupremacyculture.info/characteristics. html

Perfectionism

Perfection is linked to the characteristic of One Right Way, where there is only one right way and any deviation from this means you are failing or doing it wrong, which results in focusing on mistakes and people feeling that they are inadequate or failures. If anyone's functioning or skills falls outside of the predetermined one right way of doing things, they are immediately labelled as dysfunctional, and there is no room for acknowledging that people may simply function differently.

Either/Or Thinking

This refers to a binary way of categorizing things as good or bad, right or wrong, and it is closely connected to the One Right Way as it reinforces that any other way must be wrong. Either/Or Thinking is, again, tied to One Right Way and Perfectionism, which has led to society framing these executive functioning skills as the right skills. We frame individuals without these particular skills as dysfunctional or, worse, disordered, because we are incapable of recognizing that there are multiple ways of functioning or doing things.

Worship of the Written Word

This particular characteristic is the inability to accept information that hasn't been proven through academia or research, where the written word is prioritized over other forms of communication and where individuals with strong writing and grammatical skills are valued more than others. Our Worship of the Written Word and, consequently, academia and scientific research has led us to value executive functioning skills above all because we view executive functioning skills as the skills we all must possess. It has led to society valuing individuals who have these skills.

Quantity Over Quality

Quantity Over Quality prioritizes being able to produce measurable goals where things that can be counted or measured – such as attendance or spending money – are more highly valued than non-measurable things. As we know, executive functioning skills are skills with the purpose of meeting deadlines, making money and being productive members of society. If we didn't value quantity over quality, and our sole purpose wasn't to work and produce, what other skills could we value?

Sense of Urgency

Sense of Urgency is the idea that we must do things quickly and urgently based on arbitrary schedules that actually have little to do with how long things actually take. This ends up privileging individuals who can process information and produce work quickly. Many of the executive functioning skills come down to doing things *on demand.* We must be able to start a task immediately, which leaves no consideration for individuals who may process information at a different rate than other individuals. Similarly, it implies that everyone must have the same priorities as everyone else and we must all feel the same sense of urgency.

Fear of Open Conflict

Fear of Open Conflict results in labelling emotions as irrational, insistence on being polite, strict rules on ideas, opinions or how information should be communicated, as well as responses to discomfort that blame the individual rather than addressing the issue itself. When it comes to executive functioning skills, we expect individuals to regulate, hide or suppress their emotions regardless of the situation, even if the situation warrants it. Our society frames emotions such as anger as bad or unhealthy.

Individualism

Individualism values independence over interdependence and competition over collaboration, accountability and community. It is closely connected to One Right Way and Perfectionism. Many of the executive functioning skills expect individuals to be able to do things without any assistance or accommodations. For example, we expect people to be able to remember all of the steps of a task without assistance.

I'm the Only One

I'm the Only One is an aspect of individualism based on the belief that if something needs to get done, the individual is the only person that can do it right with no assistance or input from other individuals. We expect individuals to possess all of these executive functioning skills without realizing we all possess a wide range of skills outside of these executive functioning skills. We shouldn't expect individuals to be able to do it all themselves because we were never meant to work, achieve or function alone.

Objectivity

Objectivity assigns value to the rational and logical while believing that emotions are irrational and requiring individuals to think in a linear and logical way, while also invalidating individuals who do not think in this way. We expect individuals to be able to do things in a linear way because linear has been framed as the only way. We also frame individuals who are emotional as irrational or illogical, which leads to ignoring, dismissing and invalidating individuals just because they're expressing emotions.

Progress Is Bigger, More

Progress Is Bigger, More is connected to Quantity Over Quality and is based on the idea that success is determined by economic growth or quantity over other measures of success. If we didn't value making money or producing quantity, perhaps people would be free to do things their way even if it was at a slower pace.

Defensiveness

Defensiveness is a common response to new ideas, new ways of doing things, criticisms or objections because of Either/Or Thinking and One Right Way. Our society's tendency to respond with defensiveness has led us to reject any deviation from what we view as the one right way to function or do things. We view executive functioning skills as the one right way to function and we don't respect when individuals need to do things differently. As a result, we don't allow for new systems, new strategies or new ways.

Paternalism

Paternalism is where certain people are assigned decision-making power while the freedom and autonomy of other individuals are limited for their own good, which is determined by people in power. I think this is quite simple: society tends to take responsibilities, freedom and autonomy away from people when they do not meet expectations or standards based on the other characteristics of white supremacy.

Divergent functioning

I hope I've been able to point out the problem with executive functioning skills, so now it might be helpful to point out where we should actually go from here. Put simply, we need to get rid of the rules or, at the very least, we need to recognize that these aren't the only rules we should have to follow and stop imposing executive functioning onto neurodivergent individuals. More specifically, we need to recognize executive functioning as a set of neuronormative standards and expectations that are unrealistic for many individuals. I don't believe we can do that without unpacking, deconstructing and challenging white supremacy culture. As Tema Okun has written, we need to release white supremacy values.

We need to recognize that there is not a One Right Way of doing things but that all ways of doing things are valid and should be both respected and accommodated. We need to stop valuing perfectionism and allow individuals to make mistakes without viewing themselves as a mistake. We need to stop prioritizing individualism by prioritizing collaboration, community and working together over expecting individuals to do everything themselves without any assistance whatsoever. We need to stop basing success on producing more and doing more, where the goal is always money and profit. We need to stop expecting individuals to do things on demand just because we say so or expect so. If we can let go of white supremacy values, we can begin to realize that there are skills to be acknowledged and valued in what society calls executive dysfunction. Of course, it wouldn't really be dysfunctional just because we have different skills. What if executive functioning wasn't the norm, but, instead, creative functioning, non-linear functioning or divergent functioning?

As an Autistic ADHDer, I don't believe I lack communication skills; I just have a different way of communicating. I apply the same thinking to the way I function. I don't lack executive function skills; I just function differently with a different set of skills. I mean, do I really have trouble prioritizing or do I just have different priorities that don't revolve around being a productive member of our capitalist society? I may not be able to focus in a linear and consistent way as capitalism expects, but I can actually focus just fine in my own way; I still get things done. It just looks different. It's why we need society to both accommodate and value our divergent functioning. If society could accommodate our differences and value the way we work, think, focus, pay attention, process information and more, I truly believe that we would function in a way that works for us. We wouldn't be seen as dysfunctional. If we want to move from executive functioning to divergent functioning, what could it look like?

Executive functioning	Divergent functioning
You must be able to shift your attention from task to task immediately.	Some individuals can switch tasks easily, while other individuals experience more difficulty in switching tasks.
You must be able to sustain your focus on a task for an extended period of time.	Every individual can sustain focus on a task for different periods of time. Focus can be linear or non-linear where productivity ebbs and flows.
You must be able to complete steps in a linear fashion.	Tasks can be completed and problems can be solved creatively and non-linearly or in a step-by-step fashion.
You must be able to provide the same amount of effort for all tasks.	External and internal factors impact the effort we can provide, and we honour people's capacity where someone's value or worth isn't based on their level of effort.
You must find all tasks equally motivating regardless of your priorities, values or interests.	Every individual has differing values, priorities and interests where we do not expect individuals to conform to the same values.
You must be able to remember all the steps of a task as well as details without any assistance.	Individuals process information and memories differently, so we provide accommodations based on their needs.

cont.

Executive functioning	Divergent functioning
You must be able to start a task on demand.	People require different information, instructions or processing time before they start a task.
You must be able to structure and organize things that make sense to everyone.	Individuals structure and organize things in a way that makes sense to them.
You must have the same definition of success as everyone else.	Individuals have different definitions of success that fall outside of capitalism.
You must be able to hide or suppress your emotions, regardless of the situation.	Individuals feel and express a range of emotions because it's called being human.

As Dr Miriam Cherkes-Julkowski states in her book *The DYSfunctionality of Executive Function*, 'it is possible we have become entirely too focused on executive functioning as an end in itself, rather than as a sometimes-useful means to an end',[4] and that's what I would like everyone to take away from this: executive functioning is not the be all and end all of functioning, and it's not the only way to function. If we could move away from labelling individuals with a deficit because they do not conform to functioning a certain way, we can move towards accommodating people's differences and respecting how individuals work and function.

Emotions

When it comes to neurodivergent individuals, our emotions are

---

4   Miriam Cherkes-Julkowski, *The DYSfunctionality of Executive Function* (Apache Junction, AZ: Surviving Education Guides, 2005).

something many of us have in common when it comes to diverging from dominant societal standards and norms. Sure, we may not all diverge the exact same way, but that's just an indication of all the different ways emotional differences and emotional experiences have been labelled as abnormal, wrong or unhealthy. I also want to point out the impact and consequences of pathologizing emotions, responses and differences. Our policing of emotions has been used to justify controlling people, punishing people, justifying conservatorships, denying people their rights and even incarcerating people and silencing people. We truly need to consider if there actually is a right emotional response or even a right way to feel emotions. Or perhaps we have developed a culture of norms and expectations when it comes to our emotions.

I think the concept of labelling certain emotions as good and other emotions as bad is a prime example of how society assigns moral value to emotions. If you consider the emotions that have been labelled as bad, such as anger, sadness and frustration, it's often these emotions that are pathologized as a part of disorders.

If you consider the fact that white supremacy culture has shaped our norms, standards and values, you can see the correlation between 'bad emotions' and white supremacy; they are emotions that cause discomfort in other individuals and, of course, it's much easier to blame the individual instead of sitting with the discomfort.

One particular characteristic of white supremacy culture is fear of conflict, and it results in society framing emotions as irrational and an insistence on being polite above all else. Additionally, it tells us how we should communicate our opinions, ideas, feedback and even responses to injustice or harm. Another characteristic of white supremacy culture is objectivity. Objectivity values rationality and logic, whereas emotions are seen as irrational. As soon as someone is emotional, they're seen as irrational, lacking reason or lacking composure. I feel as though we have been conditioned to aspire to and value composure, and that if we express our emotions, it means we depart from this normal state of composure, but this isn't the case at all. If we continue to frame emotions as a problem of the individual, it allows people in power to continue to deny any wrongdoing on their behalf; it allows people in power to dismiss us purely because we are expressing emotions.

Emotional regulation

I suppose that brings us to emotional regulation which, put simply, is a process of recognizing, managing and controlling our emotions and responses to our emotions. We aren't born with the ability to regulate our emotions; our parents and our support system help us develop emotional regulation skills as we grow, learn and develop as children and teenagers. As emotional regulation is a skill that is taught, it makes sense that every individual would have varying levels of skill when it comes to regulating emotions because everyone would've been taught differently and perhaps even not taught at all. If you think about it, it's actually unfair to put the blame on the individual by labelling them with a disorder for experiencing emotional dysregulation if they didn't have access to building the skills.

I genuinely believe emotional regulation is another example of how dominant societal norms have shaped our emotional experiences because we have predetermined ideas of what emotional regulation looks like, including how individuals should actually regulate their emotions. We are expected to regulate our emotions in the right way without any consideration of internal and external differences as well as external circumstances. Are we truly expecting someone who lives in a state of constant stress and fear to be regulated all the time? Are we truly going to frame someone as disordered because they didn't have an opportunity to learn emotional regulation from their parents? Who are we genuinely helping by blaming individuals for their emotional dysregulation and framing emotional dysregulation as something to avoid or prevent or, at worst, a sign that there is something wrong with you? It's not hard to see the connection between emotional regulation and white supremacy; people become dysregulated in response to their environment, harmful systems and things that are happening to them. If we frame it as an individual problem, it is easier for society to avoid fixing the real problems that are causing people to become angry, sad or distressed. If we focus on keeping people regulated, we don't have to fix or change anything. If we classify emotional dysregulation and responses such as depression or anxiety as a part of mental disorders, it allows society to ignore the relationship between our emotions and our circumstances, environments and situations.

Candice Alaska, who runs an Instagram account providing education on BPD using an anti-oppressive and anti-capitalist lens, has invited us to 'consider the impacts of defining emotions as unacceptable or disordered, and who gets to determine what emotional experience and expression is "dysregulated", and how that can be used to harm others'.[5] I'll be honest, I don't believe anyone should be pathologized for their emotions. I also don't believe anyone is inherently abnormal, broken or wrong for having difficulty regulating their emotions or for experiencing big emotions. As Candice Alaska points out in her post, 'the idea of those being dysregulated still centres certain emotional responses as right and tells us that a certain intensity of emotions is not socially acceptable.'[6] I feel like that's what it comes down to; it's about what is considered socially or culturally acceptable, not what is actually a disorder.

5   Candice Alaska (@understandingbpd), 'I've been moving away from the language of "emotional regulation"', Instagram, 20 April 2022. www.instagram.com/p/CcjuWgSMhq3
6   Candice Alaska (@understandingbpd), 'I've been moving away from the language of "emotional regulation"', Instagram, 20 April 2022. www.instagram.com/p/CcjuWgSMhq3

Intensity of emotions

Are you someone who experiences emotions intensely? Are you someone who has been told one too many times to calm down or perhaps that you're overreacting? Like me, you might have been called 'too much' or 'too passionate' at some point. You might even be familiar with terms like 'drama queen', 'dramatic' or 'attention seeking'. It's just another example of how society frames certain emotional differences and experiences as socially unacceptable. While emotional intensity may be seen as 'socially unacceptable', it's not a bad thing at all, and it's also not a sign that something is wrong with an individual. I mean, were we really expecting individuals to feel the same way as everyone else? Where is the diversity in that? If emotions were a spectrum of colours, emotional intensity would refer to the hottest of pinks and brightest of yellows, and perhaps there are people who simply experience the boldest and brightest of emotions.

I don't believe we label people as abnormal for experiencing the emotional spectrum in a different way. If we continue to frame emotional intensity as a problem to be fixed, we won't be able to appreciate or recognize the strengths and gifts that come from experiencing emotions intensely: from love songs to heartbreak songs, from magnificent art to stories that take you far away. Can we stop telling people to calm down just because they're not following the dominant script for expressing emotions? Can we stop labelling people as dramatic or too much just because they're not following the dominant script for expressing emotions? We need to stop pathologizing individuals for experiencing and expressing emotions that fall outside of dominant societal standards and norms. We need to stop pathologizing anger, sadness, grief and frustration just because of society's tendency to avoid discomfort and conflict.

If you need another example of how Western society has determined what we consider to be socially acceptable expressions of emotions, just look at the recent addition of grief as a disorder in the DSM. It comes down to pathologizing people whose grieving doesn't follow Western society's acceptable grieving timeline and, more significantly, it comes down to pathologizing people whose grief stops them from being productive. I mean, the same goes for any other emotional experiences they've labelled as a disorder – depression, anxiety, bipolar; if it impacts our ability to be a productive member of capitalist society, if it impacts their ability to make profit off us, we are inherently the problem with a mental disorder. We really need to recognize that there aren't right or wrong ways of expressing and feeling emotions; there are just neuronormative and non-normative ways of feeling and expressing emotions or, more specifically, what is culturally and socially acceptable.

Empathy
Another example of how neuronormativity impacts our emotional experiences is our expectations when it comes to empathy. As a society, we tend to focus solely on a narrow definition of empathy that fails to account for the different kinds of empathy that exist. We tend to frame low levels of empathy as a pathology while framing higher levels of empathy as a gift or a superpower. You can tell this by how we, as a society, pathologize individuals with low empathy, yet we never tend to pathologize people with high empathy. You don't see any mental illnesses or disorders that feature high empathy as a trait, right? Individuals who don't meet society's expectations of the right level of empathy are pathologized and demonized; just look at some examples of neurodivergences such as Autism, narcissistic personality disorder (NPD) and antisocial personality disorder (ASPD), where a common feature is experiencing empathy differently.

I genuinely believe everyone experiences empathy differently, neurodivergent and neurotypical alike, and that's because there are multiple types of empathy. Basically, empathy is a complex concept that refers to the emotional and cognitive responses that occur when an individual observes another individual, where the purpose of the responses is to know what the other individual is thinking or feeling. If a friend is crying because they broke up with their partner, you may feel their sadness because you're witnessing their tears. On the other hand, you may understand what they're thinking because you remember what it was like when you went through a break-up. Those are two ways someone can experience empathy because there are actually different types of empathy. While empathy is still a developing concept, some psychologists and mental health professionals believe there are three types of empathy:

- **Emotional or affective empathy:** This is what people usually think of as empathy, and it refers to the ability to feel what someone else is feeling. When it comes to emotional empathy, you aren't feeling for them because that's sympathy; you're feeling with them or right alongside them.

- **Cognitive empathy:** Cognitive empathy is our ability to understand and know what someone is feeling or thinking by putting ourselves in their shoes. It's also called perspective taking, and it's looking at their perspective in order to understand how they might be feeling. Unlike emotional empathy, you're not feeling their feelings, but you are thinking about their feelings. I once read that cognitive empathy is why someone will rip your Band-Aid off quickly, even though it's painful, instead of peeling it off bit by bit in order to preserve your feelings.

- **Compassionate empathy:** Compassionate empathy has two components: the ability to understand what someone is going through and the motivation or urge to do something about it, whether it's solving the problem or supporting the individual in whatever way. You don't need emotional empathy in order to want to help someone either.

There are people who experience both emotional and cognitive empathy, there are people who only experience emotional empathy, and there are people who only experience cognitive empathy. Similarly, there are people who feel a high level of empathy and there are people who experience little to no empathy, and it's really important to recognize that there is no right or wrong way to experience empathy. There are also people who can experience different kinds of empathy in different contexts, where empathy can fluctuate day to day. In fact, I'm probably one of those people – any emotional and cognitive empathy I may feel is dependent on the context. However, my lack of empathy or even my difference in empathy doesn't make me a bad person or any less kind or compassionate.

I want to make the argument that empathy isn't necessary for compassion, acceptance or, you know, just being a kind person. You don't need to feel what someone else is feeling to care. You don't need to know what someone else is thinking to care. It is absolutely possible for people to be accepting or supportive of an individual without understanding their experience or feeling what they're feeling. In fact, it might even be unrealistic to expect people to be able to empathize with every individual every time, especially if we are accounting for our vast differences when it comes to gender, disability, culture, socioeconomic status and so much more. I feel that it also begs the question: is it realistic to expect every individual to experience cognitive empathy without any difficulties when so many individuals experience the world differently and yet we're supposed to make assumptions about what someone is feeling or thinking? Let's go back to my analogy of a friend going through a break-up and you're sitting next to them, okay? If we're using cognitive empathy, we are intellectualizing or analysing what they may be feeling or thinking, but the thing is, there can be a number of different ways someone might feel if they have experienced a break-up. They could be feeling regret, grief, anger, relief, fear for the future or even confusion. In fact, we can't assume and decide on one emotion to empathize with just because we've deemed it right without asking.

When it comes to feeling empathy, our default is to base our assumptions on our own processing of emotions and experiences, which may not necessarily apply to the other person's context or experience. Sure, some methods of showing support, providing comfort or problem solving could work for one individual, but they could entirely miss the mark for another individual. I suppose that brings me to my next point: we expect individuals to experience empathy because empathy is seen as the foundation of morality, and to have empathy is to act compassionately. But I beg to differ. As someone with ASPD, Bronwen (@psychopathos._) shares on Instagram their experience with having low emotional empathy: 'I don't physically feel what others around me feel, meaning that I use logic and examine body language to understand what others around me are feeling' and 'despite my low/no emotional empathy, I am just as capable to exhibit compassion and sympathy as someone with high levels; my lack of empathy doesn't mean I am incapable of showing compassion'.[7] Empathy levels are not an indication of an individual being a good or bad person. Liam, a multiply neurodivergent individual known as neurosharky, shares their

7   Bronwen (@psychopathos._), 'Empathy: My experiences', Instagram, 11 September 2022. www.instagram.com/p/CiVSeTHqBWY

experiences with empathy on an Instagram post where they explain how them having ASPD makes it nearly impossible to feel emotional empathy, while being Autistic makes it difficult for them to experience cognitive empathy because they 'simply can't read an individual's tone of voice or body language and [they] can't put [themselves] in their shoes unless [they] have known them for a long time'.[8] While Liam may struggle with both cognitive and emotional empathy, it doesn't stop them from experiencing compassionate empathy. If there is one thing we can take away from this discussion, it's that humans are diverse, so wouldn't it make sense that we are diverse in how we experience empathy, too? If we are to recognize and appreciate neurodiversity, we need to recognize diversity in empathy.

I guess I just wanna say, can we stop assuming there's a wrong way and right way to regulate our emotions and express our emotions, and can we stop assigning moral value to empathy? At the end of the day, we all see things differently, we all experience things differently and we all feel differently, and no way is this inherently bad or wrong. As David Gray-Hammond, an Autistic and mental health advocate, shares on their blog:

> We are teaching children to label their feelings as happy/sad/excited, etc., when in reality, who experiences just one simple emotion at once? How many different types of happy or sad are there? Emotion is complicated, so assuming that there is a standard experience of emotion that we should all fit into (regardless of neurotype) is not only ignorant but blatantly ableist.[9]

8 Liam (@neurosharky), 'How I experience empathy', Instagram, 20 June 2021. www.instagram.com/p/CQUKwXMMs4b

9 David Gray-Hammond, 'Creating autistic suffering: Neuronormativity in mental health treatment', Emergent Divergence, 29 January 2022. https://emergentdivergence.com/2022/01/02/creating-autistic-suffering-neuronormativity-in-mental-health-treatment

I mean, that sums it up for me: stop expecting individuals to fit into a standard experience of emotions and, most importantly, stop saying we are broken or disordered for not fitting into your box.

Communication and social norms

Many Autistic and ADHD individuals have been taught that our communication and social skills are impaired. Autistic individuals lack the ability to adjust our behaviour to suit different social contexts or situations. ADHDers can't sit still and talk too fast by jumping from topic to topic. Similarly, Autistic people communicate in a way that is blunt and straight to the point, refusing to believe that it is more important to lie or spare someone's feelings rather than say what we are actually thinking. We aren't impaired, though; we're just communicating and socializing differently. Damien Milton, an Autistic academic, author and consultant, explains this phenomenon as the double empathy problem in a significant research piece that, in summary, demonstrates how Autistic people aren't actually impaired; we are experiencing differences. Milton explains the double empathy problem as a 'breach in the natural attitude that occurs between people of different dispositional outlooks and personal conceptual understandings when attempts are made to communicate meaning'.[10] See, it is a 'double problem' because it isn't necessarily a problem with one individual but a mismatch in individuals who hold different norms and expectations of each other. As Milton describes it, Autistic people may lack insight into the minds and cultures of non-Autistic people, but the same applies for non-Autistic people; they also lack insight into the minds and cultures of Autistic people, but never say non-Autistic people

10   Damian E.M. Milton, 'On the ontological status of autism: The "double empathy problem"', *Disability and Society* 27, no. 6 (2012): 883–887. https://doi.org/10.1080 /09687599.2012.710008

have impaired social and communication skills. I want to share a great analogy by Jillian Enright, who is a neurodivergent writer:

> If you had a room full of only-French and only-English speaking people, would people not communicate better with those who speak the same language? If the majority of the people were French-speaking, would we consider the English-speaking people deficient? Or would we understand that a language barrier was to blame, not any individual person, or particular group of people? What Autistics encounter when trying to communicate with neuro-typicals are cultural and neurodivergence barriers: it's two people – or groups of people – who communicate in very different ways. It's just been assumed that neurotypical communication styles are superior, because they're the majority.[11]

Basically, there isn't one right way of communicating or socializing; there's only a culturally and socially dominant way of communicating and socializing that is no less right or wrong than the non-dominant way. You've probably heard Autistic people say how it feels as though we're missing the social rulebook that is given to everyone except us, and honestly, it is a very accurate analogy because these communication and social norms often act as a set of rules on how we must communicate and socialize within society. As I mentioned earlier in this chapter, norms and rules exist to achieve a goal, a purpose or some kind of desired result. Well, our social and communication norms are no different – the goal is to achieve social cohesion. While there are a number of different definitions of what social cohesion means, there is a common feature to all the definitions: it is a set of shared values, norms or processes that

11   Jillian Enright, 'Defining neurotypical privilege', Medium, 14 December 2021. https://medium.com/neurodiversified/neurotypical-privilege-690f0e14d370

provide a sense of belonging, where individuals feel that they are members of the same community.

You might be asking, why is all of this important? Well, I believe if we want to move towards a more neurodiversity-affirming society where neurodivergent individuals aren't pathologized or seen as having deficits, we need to challenge the status quo of communication and social norms. If we want to challenge these norms, we should probably figure out what they actually are and where on earth they come from. It's my pleasure to announce that I tried really, really hard to identify some common social and communication norms. Unsurprisingly, I couldn't find a definitive list on the internet, but after some research into social and communication 'deficits' and exploring the type of social and communication skills that Autistic children are taught, there were both some subtle and obvious norms disguised in there. Once again, unsurprisingly, you'll find that a lot of these norms uphold white supremacy culture.

You must express an appropriate amount of emotion through verbal and non-verbal body language when communicating

I've often been told to calm down when having a conversation with someone, even if I wasn't particularly upset, just because I was unable to control the tone of my voice. It was actually the biggest relief for me when I found friends who I could communicate with without having to worry they'd misinterpret my tone of voice or tell me to tone it down. On the other side of things, I've even been accused of appearing standoffish because of my lack of facial expression or I've been told I need to sound more appropriate or say things in a nicer way. One specific example happened last year where I was in a group setting and I was talking passionately with someone else; our voices were both raised because of our interest in the topic. One of the staff members came over to make sure we were both all right because it looked as though we were arguing.

See, the person made an assumption based on how we were talking, including our tone of voice. There is an expectation within society to always show an appropriate amount of emotion during a conversation – you need to adapt your facial expressions to match the context, you need to adjust your tone of voice according to your intent. If you speak too loudly, it's a sign you're getting angry or aggressive. If you stand with your hands on your hips, it's a sign you're impatient or angry.

Autistic Science Person, in their blog, says there are three assumptions that neurotypical people make when it comes to tone of voice, and I believe they can also be seen as a set of communication norms:

1. Everyone who speaks or vocalizes is trying to 'send a message' based on how their voice sounds. This includes timbre, pitch, loudness, etc.

2. Everyone who speaks or vocalizes can control their voice with ease – i.e. can change their timbre/pitch/loudness very easily.

3. Everyone who speaks or vocalizes knows exactly what their voice is actually doing while they're speaking (whether it 'sounds defensive' or sounds loud or quiet, etc.).[12]

You must be able to assume or interpret someone's feelings and intentions by their tone of voice

In a way, it's a bit ridiculous that we expect that everyone who speaks is trying to send a message with how they're talking or

---

[12] Autistic Science Person, 'Neurotypicals: Listen to our words, not our tone', blog post, 9 January 2021. https://autisticscienceperson.com/2021/01/09/neurotypicals-listen-to-our-words-not-our-tone

sounding. Quite frankly, it's unfair to apply the same assumptions and interpretations to every individual when everyone is different, not just with their tone of voice but the simple fact that everyone has their own meanings and their own experiences. Does anyone actually believe we can make an accurate assumption about someone's feelings or intentions just by their tone of voice? One of the most important things we can learn to do is to listen to a person's words, not their tone of voice. I've repeatedly had to state to people that I say what I mean and I mean what I say; there's no subtext or hidden meaning. Often, people will say I'm feeling defensive or angry when I'm responding to someone and come across as blunt. Perhaps if we listen to what someone is saying, we will spend less time trying to analyse how they're saying it and we can finally let go of all the guesswork.

It is important to make eye contact to demonstrate to someone that you are paying attention and are interested in what they are saying

When it comes to making eye contact, this is a social and communication norm because there is a set of assumptions, rules or beliefs surrounding it. In Western society, we believe making eye contact is a sign of respect, a sign of interest, and it demonstrates that you're paying attention. If you don't make eye contact, people believe you're distracted, rude, uninterested and even untrustworthy. I want to put this simply: making eye contact is merely a social norm, and yet individuals who struggle to make eye contact are pathologized and labelled as 'abnormal' or unwell. Are we really assuming that individuals have a disorder just because they don't follow social norms? We really need to stop making assumptions about what people's lack of eye contact might mean and stop assigning arbitrary rules around making eye contact. I may not make eye contact, but it doesn't mean I'm not paying attention and it doesn't mean I'm not interested; it just means I'm not making eye contact.

You cannot interrupt someone when they're talking, as it is perceived as rude

I feel like this is a very obvious norm – one we've probably all heard our entire lives. Interrupting someone when they're talking is against the rules because it's rude. There are definitely individuals who do feel hurt or maybe even frustrated by being interrupted, but the thing is, it's actually not everyone who feels frustrated or hurt by it – in fact, interrupting is a natural way to communicate in a conversation and neither individual sees it as rude. I don't think it's accurate to say that interrupting is rude when it isn't everyone who finds it rude. It's actually centring the individuals who do find it rude without considering that other communication styles exist.

It is important to prioritize another person's comfort when providing feedback, correcting someone, answering a question or communicating information

It's an unspoken rule that we must provide feedback, criticism, corrections and answers in a way that is padded with niceties or, in other words, sugarcoated. Autistic Science Person, in their blog, wrote about this after a discussion with non-Autistic people who claimed there was an obvious but unspoken boundary between 'brutally honest' and a 'better version of honesty', but the thing is, 'this notion of clear boundaries between those things can be thrown out the window entirely due to allistic people's negative interpretations of autistic body language and tone of voice'.[13] Similarly, this particular communication and social norm is a big part of

13 Autistic Science Person, 'Be honest: Autistic vs neurotypical honesty', blog post, 17 May 2021. https://autisticscienceperson.com/2021/05/17/be-honest-au-tistic-vs-neurotypical-honesty

professionalism; it is unprofessional to correct someone who has a higher position than you. It reminds me of a compliment sandwich where you phrase criticism or feedback in a way that starts and ends with a compliment. It's all about making sure the other person is comfortable, regardless of the situation or context.

I've heard so many similar stories from Autistic individuals who have been asked a question such as 'Do you like my new haircut?' by a friend, family member, classmate or co-worker, and despite answering honestly with 'Not really', they've been met with anger. Apparently, when individuals ask someone a question like this, they're more interested in validation than actual honesty, but the thing is, is it fair to expect individuals to lie to preserve someone's feelings or is it better to recognize that everyone has different preferences when it comes to hairstyles and we can take validation from the fact that we like our own haircut and that's all that matters? If we ask someone a question, we should expect honesty, and if we want validation, we should simply ask for it. I actually had an interaction with an Autistic friend once where I was freaking out over an overseas holiday, and I just really needed reassurance and a healthy dose of certainty. Instead of relying on them to give me validation by picking up on my obvious anxiety, I actually asked them to tell me everything was going to be okay and it was all going to work out, even if they didn't know it was going to work out. Sure, I knew they were lying, but I didn't need honesty in that particular situation; I just needed external validation, and by asking for it, I received it.

It is expected that every conversation is a reciprocal conversation which begins with small talk

Quite frankly, I've never been good at pretending I'm interested in something I'm not, and I don't understand the point of faking interest in something because I would be doing a disservice to myself and the other person. It's why I struggle with small talk and reciprocal conversation, which is like playing a game of catch by throwing a ball back and forth but instead the ball is a question you take turns asking and answering. Basically, a reciprocal conversation means stating or asking something with the expectation that you will receive a response from the other person. What if we can't think of a question, though? What if we're not interested in the topic so we genuinely don't want to ask anything about it? I guess it's what they call 'social deficits', but really, I'm just not willing to fake it.

Janae Elisabeth, a neurodiversity advocate, explained how Autistic people have our own set of social rules:

> We don't do small talk. We enjoy parallel play and shared activities that don't require continual conversation. When we talk, it gets deep quickly. We discuss what's real, our struggles, fears, desires, obsessions. We appreciate a good infodump, and there's no such thing as oversharing. We swap SAME stories – sharing a time when we felt similarly in our own life, not as a competition, but to reflect how well we are listening to each other.[14]

Spoken communication is the superior and default form of communication

I think it's extremely important to acknowledge that many of the previous communication and social norms we've discussed also rely on one particular norm: that spoken communication is the superior and default form of communication. Since white supremacy culture values the written word, and society views spoken communication as superior, it is clear that society's ideal person is someone who

14 Trauma Geek, 'Lost in translation: The social language theory of neurodivergence (part 1 of 2)', Medium, 24 May 2020. https://autietraumageek.medium.com/lost-in-translation-the-social-language-theory-of-neurodivergence-part-1-of-2-1963ba0073c5

writes and speaks well. If someone doesn't use spoken communication or uses spoken communication unreliably, people make assumptions that someone cannot think or understand if they do not speak or even that they're not competent. However, just because an individual doesn't communicate through speaking doesn't mean they do not communicate at all; they communicate differently. As a non-speaking Autistic advocate shares:

> there is so much value put on oral vocal speech, (mouth words) that people not only overlook but also devalue any other method of communication... [This has led] to hundreds of thousands of people being denied communication access, or forced to wait years before anyone tried to start to find a method of communication that worked for them, spending years fighting to have their voice heard, and having their other forms of communication often looked at as problematic behaviour.[15]

I'm sure this isn't a complete list of social and communication norms, but it's definitely a start, so why do these norms exist and where did they come from? Well, these particular norms are cultural norms and, more specifically, Western cultural norms. If we really examine these norms and why they may exist, it all comes down to upholding white supremacy culture. If you remember the white supremacy characteristic Fear of Conflict, you can actually see how a number of these communication and social norms are rules for how ideas, differences of opinion or information should be communicated with the insistence on being polite above honesty. Karla Thomas, a Black writer and activist, discusses the need to stop centring white cultural norms and feelings in an article about call-out

---

15 Autistic AAC Underground, 'There is more to speaking than vocal oral speech', blog post, 1 November 2019. https://autisticaacunderground.blogspot.com/2019/11/there-is-more-to-speaking-than-vocal.html

culture and says this: 'Bottling up feelings or only communicating them when it's convenient, polite and socially acceptable is a norm to white culture and some Asian cultures. I invite you to consider for a moment that white culture is not the gold standard.'[16] Even as I'm writing this, I'm trying to figure out how to phrase this in a way that is polite and palatable because I'm well aware that people receive information more readily when they feel comfortable, but the thing is, it isn't actually my job to make you or anyone else reading this feel comfortable, so I'm going to go ahead and say it: politeness is a tool of oppression.

It is used to prevent employees from speaking up against their bosses and managers, even when their words are completely valid. It is used against Black people and especially Black women by labelling them as angry or rude when they speak up against oppression. When it comes to white supremacy culture, the only acceptable dialogue is dialogue that doesn't make people uncomfortable. I'm not saying we should start saying whatever we like and ignore people's feelings, but maybe it shouldn't be a blanket rule to prioritize people's comfort over facts or honesty when sharing feedback, criticism or an opinion. Perhaps we need to recognize that discomfort isn't necessarily a bad thing, and it isn't always the responsibility of the other individual to avoid our discomfort. Instead, it is our responsibility to sit with the discomfort and figure out what our discomfort is actually telling us.

There's another insidious impact of our obsession with politeness. Centring other people's comfort has led to us ignoring our own needs and comfort. We're expected to make eye contact even if we find it uncomfortable or it makes it harder to focus. We're

---

16 Karla Thomas, 'Mad about call-out culture? Stop centering white cultural norms & feelings', Medium, Quad-Rants 4 Change, 26 August 2019. https://medium.com/quad-rants-4-change/mad-about-call-out-culture-stop-centering-white-cultural-norms-feelings-94335095e007

expected to sit still and display the appropriate body language even though our bodies move in different ways. We're expected to maintain interest in a conversation while 'umming' and 'ahhing' at the appropriate times, even though we may be exhausted, distracted or simply not interested. We're even expected to remain involved in a conversation at a dinner party because if we're caught reading a book or scrolling our phone, it's seen as rude even when we don't have the energy to participate. Putting Autistic children through social skills is a classic example of teaching someone to ignore their needs and bodies. I remember seeing in one particular social skills programme an instruction that says something like this: 'Think about what your body looks like. Are you making others have good thoughts or bad thoughts? If you are making others have bad thoughts, adjust your body.' I mean, there are two problems with this: first, it doesn't consider the fact that everyone has different needs or different ways of moving and, second, how on earth do they expect us to know whether someone is having good thoughts or bad thoughts? It would require mindreading, and basing it on assumptions is a fool's game. Once again, we are centring other people's comfort by having to be responsible for the thoughts other people may have and adjusting our bodies accordingly.

In fact, we are expected to participate in a conversation and appear interested by asking questions because it's the polite thing to do. I mentioned earlier that I've never been good at pretending to be interested in something; if I'm not interested, I'm not interested, you know? I'm not uncaring; I'm just genuine. In fact, I would assume it's rude rather than polite to pretend and fake your way through a conversation. Are we really expecting people to be disingenuous in the name of being polite? Have you ever been labelled antisocial, a party pooper, a loser or even a downer because you didn't show the appropriate amount of enthusiasm at a party or you were sitting out of a party game or hiding in a corner? That's another example of how we expect individuals to ignore their needs in order to socialize and uphold this idea of what it means to be polite. In an article on Medium called 'Most social norms are arbitrary', Jillian Enright shares their experience from a family gathering:

> There were 10 adults and eight children all running around, swimming, playing, doing cottage-y things. It was a lot of fun accompanied by a lot of noise and activity. I used to push myself to do *all* of the obligatory adulting and would end up burnt out and irritable. Now I understand myself better, I am also much better equipped to advocate for my own needs, and to be honest about who I am and what I enjoy. My in-laws understand and know me well enough to know that if I go off to read on my own, it's because that's what I want and need at that time, not because I don't enjoy their company.[17]

Jillian Enright made an excellent point after sharing her story: 'Perhaps the issue is people taking the behaviour of others personally, rather than considering that everybody's social and sensory needs are different.'[18] Perhaps that's what it boils down to, really. Our society expects every individual to communicate in the same way, but it is an unfair expectation that privileges individuals who can communicate in the dominant way while other individuals who communicate differently are ostracized, excluded and labelled with a disorder. As Janae Elisabeth has so eloquently put it, 'the set of traits that Western society has decided is normal is terribly

17 Jillian Enright, 'Most social norms are arbitrary', Medium, neurodiversified, 6 September 2022. https://medium.com/neurodiversified/most-social-norms-are-arbitrary-283db0b477af

18 Jillian Enright, 'Most social norms are arbitrary', Medium, neurodiversified, 6 September 2022. https://medium.com/neurodiversified/most-social-norms-are-arbitrary-283db0b477af

unrealistic for our neurotype',[19] and to add to that, it's unrealistic for every neurodivergent person. These norms end up imposing a sense of shame whenever we fall short of their expectations, and it's not just neurodivergent individuals who feel the shame but every individual, too. I don't think it's just neurodivergent individuals who have pushed through a social event even if they weren't feeling up to it. I don't think it's just neurodivergent individuals who have spent hours reliving every conversation where they talked too much or said the wrong thing. I don't think it's just neurodivergent individuals who have remained silent instead of sharing what they really thought or felt. I'm sure everyone has ended up ignoring their needs in order to be polite once, twice or many times in their lives. In fact, I believe challenging these communication and social norms will better serve most, if not, all individuals, neurodivergent and neurotypical people alike.

I read an article called 'Being Over Polite Is Dangerously Bad for You' by Charlie Brown, a British writer, who moved to Spain from the UK and realized 'how redundant, annoying and frankly bad for me much of my politeness was'. Charlie found that, in Spain, 'everyone simply stated what they wanted to do and a consensus was made either based on the majority, or with compromises. It worked because no one was expecting false politeness and no one got huffy with differing opinions'.[20] I think it would absolutely be a game changer if we stopped expecting false politeness and began to accept that everyone has differing opinions, needs and communication

---

19 Trauma Geek, 'Lost in translation: The social language theory of neurodivergence (part 1 of 2)', Medium, 24 May 2020. https://autietraumageek.medium.com/lost-in-translation-the-social-language-theory-of-neurodivergence-part-1-of-2-1963ba0073c5

20 Charlie Brown, 'Being over polite is dangerously bad for you. Here are 6 reasons (and ways) to stop now', Medium, Mind Café, 26 July 2022). https://medium.com/mind-cafe/being-over-polite-is-dangerously-bad-for-you-here-are-6-reasons-and-ways-to-stop-now-1c0f4e4a4743

styles. In order to do that, we need other individuals to stop perceiving differing opinions, needs and communication styles as rude or a personal affront. We need to stop ignoring our needs and comfort in the name of politeness. We need to stop ignoring our own opinions and ideas in the name of politeness.

I'm totally aware that we're not going to get rid of communication and social norms overnight, and quite possibly these communications and social norms will remain within society, but ideally they won't be a set of rules that every individual must follow. We can, instead, move forward by teaching individuals these particular communication and social norms without the expectation that they are a requirement. And hey, you've got to know about the rules in order to break the rules, and that's exactly what we want here – to break free from these communication and social rules. We need to move away from labelling someone with a disorder just because they don't communicate or socialize according to these dominant norms. We need to acknowledge that there are different forms of communication where one is no more valid than the other. We need to recognize that communicating or socializing differently doesn't mean there is anything wrong with us.

Learning

As you now know, the term 'neurodivergent' refers to any individual who has a mind or brain that diverges from dominant societal standards and norms; and it includes ways of learning that fall outside what society deems 'normal'. Of course, when we say normal, we actually mean the dominant ways of learning because, in Western society, there's only one 'right way' to learn, and it's got a lot to do with capitalism and white supremacy. In order to understand why learning differences are seen as learning disorders or deficits in the eyes of Western society, it's important to understand what

Western society values – reading, writing and mathematics. I'm sure you can see the correlation: people with dyslexia have difficulty with reading, people with dysgraphia have difficulty with writing, and people with dyscalculia have difficulty with mathematics. Basically, it's only because Western society views reading, writing and mathematics as the pinnacle of learning, intelligence and success that the Pathology Paradigm frames individuals who learn differently as having deficits or having disorders.

I guess you're wondering what reading, writing and mathematics has to do with capitalism and white supremacy, and honestly, the answer is a lot. You've probably noticed throughout this chapter that capitalism and white supremacy have shaped our dominant societal standards and norms, and alas, education, learning and teaching are no exception. In fact, it was kind of the whole reasoning behind developing the Western education system and compulsory schooling. Capitalism was on the rise, so schools became a way of ensuring that every individual had the minimum knowledge to be employable, and, of course, reading and writing were the knowledge needed to be employable in the workforce.[21] If you think about it, the worst place you can make a spelling mistake is on your résumé or cover letter because it's seen as a lack of intelligence or the sign of a poor worker, which is obviously untrue as well as ableist. But I digress. Another part of the Western education system was teaching individuals to become productive members of society through rules, norms and expectations, including respect for authority, competition, individualism and compliance. You just have to look at the structure of classrooms: long hours, minimal breaks, grades, assessments, authorized texts, bells and even just having to sit in rows of chairs while facing the front of the room

---

21 Faolan Jones, 'The colonial roots of educational inequity', liberate.ed, 3 April 2020. https://liberate-ed.com/2020/04/03/the-colonial-roots-of-educational-inequity

where a teacher instructs you. I mean, that's what it comes down to, really, because as Alfie Kohn writes: 'We must never forget the primary reason that children attend school – namely, to be trained in the skills that will maximize the profits earned by their future employers.'[22]

On the more insidious side of things, the introduction of the Western education system had the purpose of assimilating individuals into the ideology of white supremacy by erasing their Indigenous history, knowledge and ways.[23] As John Southard writes: 'Colonial education strips the colonized people away from their indigenous learning structures and draws them toward the structures of the colonizers.'[24] It's evident by the mere fact that curriculums teach Western science which values data and measurements over Indigenous knowledge, which values nature, creativity and storytelling. Dr Aleryk Fricker, a Dja Dja Warring man and school teacher, shares that prior to colonization, First Nations people had wonderful, complex and effective methods of teaching and learning for their children and communities, but with the invasion of Australia and the ongoing genocide of First Nations people, their methods of learning and teaching have been significantly disrupted and removed. It's still evident to this day; there's a reason that teaching and learning focuses on reading and writing over the ways First Nations learn such as yarning, art and Dreamtime stories.[25] It doesn't

22 Alfie Kohn, 'When "21st-century schooling" just isn't good enough: A modest proposal', Alfie Kohn, 18 November 2014. www.alfiekohn.org/article/21st-century-schooling-just-isn't-good-enough-modest-proposal

23 Faolan Jones, 'The colonial roots of educational inequity', liberate.ed, 3 April 2020. https://liberate-ed.com/2020/04/03/the-colonial-roots-of-educational-inequity

24 John Southard, 'Colonial education', Scholar Blogs, October 2017. https://scholarblogs.emory.edu/postcolonialstudies/2014/06/20/colonial-education

25 Fricker Aleryk, 'Decolonising your classroom: Five ways forward', AEU News, 9 October 2021. https://news.aeuvic.asn.au/in-depth/decolonising-your-classroom-five-ways-forward

have to be this way, though, and, in fact, in New Zealand, they're actually challenging the Western style of education by introducing oral and verbal learning because in Māori culture, their stories, knowledge and history are passed down through generations orally.

When it comes to white supremacy culture influencing norms around learning, we need to consider how white supremacy values the worship of the written word. This has shaped what Western society values, and that's individuals with strong writing and grammatical skills. Put simply, there is an expectation that individuals must be able to read and write to a certain standard because, as Tema Okun puts it, 'if it's not grammatically "correct", it has no value'.[26] When it comes to difficulties with reading, writing and mathematics, it is seen as a disorder because it goes against what Western society views as a functional, intelligent and productive individual. I mean, I'm terrible at learning dances – it's simply something I struggle with, but no one would say I have a disorder because I can't learn to dance. I've also always struggled to learn an instrument or paint well; again, nobody has ever said that's a disorder, and that's because society values the skills that will make an individual be a productive member of our capitalist society, and we do not view art, music or dance as contributing to capitalism.

I'm not saying writing, reading and maths aren't important or useful skills, especially in a society where writing, reading and maths are often necessary, but I am saying we shouldn't assume an individual is abnormal or unwell because they may not have these particular skills. When we frame these skills as the most important skills to have, we miss out on valuing every other skill. On a similar note, we need to move away from expecting individuals to learn in a particular way or express their knowledge in a particular way. If we continue to frame writing essays and passing written tests

---

26 Tema Okun, 'Characteristics', White supremacy culture characteristics.' Accessed 28 October 2022. www.whitesupremacyculture.info/characteristics.html

as the only way of knowing something, we are missing out on all the other ways of knowing from oral storytelling, singing, dancing, art and movement. At the end of the day, there are visual learners, auditory learners, verbal learners, physical learners, social learners and solitary learners. It isn't the individual who learns differently that's the problem, it's the fact that our education system and class-rooms are set up in such a rigid way that they only support individuals who learn in a particular way.

Time

I wasn't sure how I was going to approach this particular topic, only that I knew I really wanted to because as an Autistic ADHDer with bipolar, my relationship to time has always been unique and, consequently, has always been pathologized by society. As time is a social construct, it makes sense that there are societal standards and norms when it comes to time. Just like every other norm or standard that individuals often diverge from, time is no different. As someone with bipolar, my relationship with time and how I perceive time actually changes; it's actually what leads to me experiencing manic episodes. While most individuals associate mania with a shift in our mood, it's actually also a shift in our perception of time.[27] In order to understand this, it might be helpful to consider that there are two types of time: world time, or clock time, and our internal sense of time – you could call it our internal clock. I want to share a quote from Virginia Woolf's novel *Orlando*:

> An hour, once it lodges in the queer element of the human spirit, may be stretched to fifty or a hundred times its clock length; on the

27 Marcin Moskalewicz and Michael A. Schwartz, 'Temporal experience in mania', *Phenomenology and the Cognitive Sciences* 19, no. 2 (2018): 291–304. https://doi.org/10.1007/s11097-018-9564-0

other hand, an hour may be accurately represented by the time-piece of the mind by one second. This extraordinary discrepancy between time on the clock and time in the mind is less known than it should be, and deserves fuller investigation.[28]

Virginia Woolf was right in saying that it needs to be well known that there is discrepancy between how an individual experiences time versus the time on the clock. While we can definitely agree on how many hours have passed if we look at the clock, how that particular time has passed will feel different for each individual. When it comes to individuals experiencing mania, our internal clock speeds up so that our inner sense of time and world time do not match up – our internal clock is basically existing at a different tempo.[29] It's not just individuals with bipolar who experience differences with their internal clock either. ADHDers also have a faster inner clock, too, and there are studies[30] that show that individuals with schizophrenia have an internal clock that speeds up, slows down and doesn't necessarily run at a constant speed. Many individuals with schizophrenia report that they often feel as though time is running slower or faster, while other individuals often say they cannot sense what time, day or month it is.[31] I don't believe

28 Virginia Woolf, *Orlando* (London: Penguin, 2011).

29 Georg Northoff, Paola Magioncalda, Matteo Martino, Hsin-Chien Lee, Ying-Chi Tseng and Timothy Lane, 'Too fast or too slow? Time and neuronal variability in bipolar disorder – a combined theoretical and empirical investigation', *Schizophrenia Bulletin* 44, no. 1 (2017): 54–64. https://doi.org/10.1093/schbul/sbx050

30 Giovanni Stanghellini, Massimo Ballerini, Simona Presenza, Milena Mancini, Andrea Raballo, Stefano Blasi and John Cutting, 'Psychopathology of lived time: Abnormal time experience in persons with schizophrenia', Schizophrenia Bulletin 42, no. 1 (January 2016): 45–55. https://doi.org/10.1093/schbul/sbv052; hilalkatirci, 'Time perception in schizophrenia: Do schizophrenic patients perceive time differently?' Brainy Sundays, 14 December 2019. https://scanberlin.com/2019/12/15/time-perception-in-schizophrenia-do-schizophrenic-patients-perceive-time-differently

31 Giovanni Stanghellini, Massimo Ballerini, Simona Presenza, Milena Mancini, Andrea Raballo, Stefano Blasi and John Cutting, 'Psychopathology of lived time: Abnormal time experience in persons with schizophrenia', Schizophrenia Bulletin 42, no. 1 (January 2016): 45–55. https://doi.org/10.1093/schbul/sbv052

anyone can sense what time, day or month it is; we are merely told what time, day or month it is. We rely on world time or clock time. I mean, our inner clocks aren't Swiss-made watches, you know?

In fact, neurodivergent individuals aren't the only people who can experience time differently. Western cultures view time as a linear state divided into past, present and future, where time can be measured and managed. As time is something that can be wasted or used efficiently, schedules and punctuality are important. However, not everyone actually views time in the same way. When it comes to how time is perceived and valued, different cultures have different experiences with time. For example, in Native American cultures as well as African cultures, time is viewed as flexible; relationships are more important than schedules, and time is connected to our natural rhythms. In Australia, First Nations people view time as procedural where time is relational and revolves around events, activities and personal meaning. It's actually similar to how ADHDers experience time; we don't view time as a linear sequence but as a collection of events that are connected to people, emotions and activities.[32]

It might be helpful to know that we haven't always viewed time as a linear, unidirectional concept. In fact, we moved from a cyclical concept of time to a linear concept of time because of the industrial era and, more specifically, the development of capitalism. As Marta explains on Instagram, 'This construct isn't any sort of real or natural time. This is time as it has been imposed on us by industrial capitalism, fuelled by white supremacy.'[33] In fact, many countries and cultures were reluctant to embrace the world clock and

32 hilalkatirci, 'Time perception in schizophrenia: Do schizophrenic patients perceive time differently?' Brainy Sundays, 14 December 2019. https://scanberlin. com/2019/12/15/time-perception-in-schizophrenia-do-schizophrenic-patients-perceive-time-differently
33 Divergent Design Studios (@divergent_design_studio), 'Industrial time is a social construct', Instagram, 3 April 2021. www.instagram.com/p/CNN2GRvsJKT

only did so because of the demands of capitalism and commerce. Our norms around time are due to values of the dominant society and, like many other norms, it's all about valuing capitalism. I mean, it's much easier to enforce a nine-to-five, five-days-a-week work schedule when we view time as a linear progression where every moment counts.

If we can acknowledge that everyone perceives time differently, and our dominant concept of time isn't the only concept of time but a standard or norm fuelled by capitalism, why are we labelling individuals who perceive time differently as abnormal? If everyone perceives time differently, how can it actually be wrong? Well, it's because what we label as 'abnormal' just means it doesn't fit into Western society's concept of linear time. As Kama Jensen shares in an article on Attitude:

> You're not really horrible with time. You just have a unique and un-appreciated way of interacting with the physical world. Your time awareness and task management doesn't follow neurotypical pat-terns, but that doesn't mean there is anything inherently wrong with you.[34]

I don't believe we're broken, wrong or abnormal just because our inner clock or how we perceive time simply doesn't match the dominant sense of time. Can we move away from pathologizing this difference and, instead, recognize it as another way that many individuals diverge from dominant societal norms and standards? Maybe if we could adjust our immediate environment and our external time to our personal inner time, we would feel less wrong.

34 Kama Jensen, 'Your concept of time is not broken, it's just unorthodox', ADDitude, 10 December 2020. www.additudemag.com/concept-of-time-differs-adhd-brains

Perhaps our shift in time wouldn't cause such a desynchronization because we're forcing ourselves to function according to a world clock that doesn't match our own inner clock. I mean, the Doctor from *Doctor Who* was correct when they said, 'People assume that time is a strict progression from cause to effect, but actually from a non-linear, non-subjective viewpoint, it's more like a big ball of wibbly wobbly, timey wimey...stuff.'[35] Our time was never supposed to be linear with a strict progression; capitalism made it that way.

Plurality

Plurality, or multiplicity, is the existence of multiple selves or entities within a single physical body. According to the Plural Association, plurality is an umbrella term that encompasses all experiences of being or having more than a single individual within a single body, regardless of words or labels used to describe these sorts of individual experiences.[36] You might be familiar with dissociative identity disorder (DID) or other specified dissociative disorder (OSDD); while these are experiences of plurality, not all plural systems identify with these terms. As Anthony Temple writes in their article titled 'Multiplicity is natural', the continuous framing of plurality or multiplicity as a disorder or pathology 'implies that multiplicity is damage, that it is intrinsically wrong; that being single is normal and multiplicity is abnormal',[37] which is why many plural systems are moving away from identifying with these terms that are pathologizing and moving towards terms that focus on plurality as an identity or experience.

35 www.youtube.com/watch?v=q2nNzNo_Xps
36 The Plural Association, 'Plurality'. Accessed 16 June 2022, https://powertotheplurals.com/glossary/plurality
37 Anthony Temple, 'Multiplicity is natural'. Accessed 4 September 2022, http://astraeasweb.net/plural/theory.html

I would like to offer the suggestion that the entire concept of a singular self is actually another neuronormative norm or social construct. See, the idea that one body has one person or one personality or one mind isn't necessarily a scientific concept but a cultural concept or social norm. As The Rings System shares on Twitter:

> Plurality challenges the dominant western societal conceptualization of personhood as single & autonomous – it queers how our bodies are seen as an extension of ourselves, how our bodies are used to express ourselves, how our bodies are seen as representative of ourselves.[38]

Meg-John Barker, author of a number of popular books, shares on their website Rewriting the Rules that, in a way, the concept of the singular self is an invention of capitalism. In a discussion between two of their plural selves, they write this:

> We're all pressured to tell stories of our self as if we were consistent and coherent when actually we're all complex and contradictory. You could even go so far as to say that experiencing yourself as utterly singular is the 'crazy' thing, and that trying to present yourself in that way does quite a violence to yourself. Certainly many indigenous cultures have understandings of selfhood that encompass plurality and would see the idea of a singular self as weird or unlikely.[39]

If you think about it, we all play different roles in different parts

38 The Rings System, 'Plurality challenges the dominant western societal conceptualization of personhood as single & autonomous – it queers how our bodies are seen as an extension of ourselves, how our bodies are used to express ourselves, how our bodies are seen as representative of ourselves', Twitter, 23 September 2021. https://twitter.com/TheRingsSystem/status/1441057390695223297
39 Meg-John Barker, 'Plural Selves FAQ', Rewriting the Rules, 14 August 2020. www.rewriting-the-rules.com/self/plural-selves-faq

of our lives – who we are at work might be different from who we are at home. Similarly, we may all show different sides of ourselves when it comes to which friends we are hanging out with. I'm sure many of you have been in two minds about something, where one part of you wants to stay home while another part of you wants to go out with friends, or one part of you wants to study law while another part of you wants to study art. I want to make it clear that recognizing we all have parts of ourselves isn't the same as the plurality or multiplicity experience. While there is overlap, they are vastly different experiences, but I wanted to offer these examples to demonstrate the normality of these experiences.

Sarah K Reece, a diversity and inclusion specialist who identifies as multiple/plural, shares a similar sentiment:

> There's a theory about the 'self' which states that who you are is not a fixed thing, like a rock or a plant. It's a unique dynamic. That 'self' is what emerges in relationship with another. So each 'self' in each setting, each relationship, is slightly unique, and has aspects that may differ from all others. This is both separate to and part of multiplicity. I experience this in both which parts are brought out and also the different selves we all have. This is an aspect of multiplicity which is universal to all of us.[40]

In order to recognize all the plural experiences including DID and OSDD as neurodivergent, we need to recognize plurality as another way of being human, another way of existing in this world. As Anthony Temple shares on Astraeas Web, 'We don't have a mental disorder; we're multiple, that's not a mental disorder. It's a psychoneurological fact. A household can be in disarray, members

---

40 Sarah K Reece, 'We are all multiple, and so are the people who hurt us', Sarah K Reece, 10 July 2019. https://sarahkreece.com/2019/07/10/we-are-all-multiple-and-so-are-the-people-who-hurt-us

of a household can have emotional problems, but multiplicity it-self is not a disorder.'[41] While plural systems and multiple systems may diverge from this idea of the singular person being the norm, it doesn't mean they need to be fixed by becoming singular. Anthony Temple states, 'The entire idea that a multiple group must "integrate" in this sense is a product of social control through rigid definition'[42] of the right way to be a person where the only valid identity is a singular identity. It's not to say there's no distress or challenges, but perhaps the solution doesn't revolve around blaming or fixing the plurality or multiplicity. Astraea shares on Astraea's Web, 'Whether the *we* is a wrong thing, something that should not be, a brokenness that is healed only by flowing back into the One, *that should be for the client and their group to decide*, not some singlet who's never been multiple and cannot know what it is like.'[43]

Just like the rest of this chapter, this is about challenging our concept of normal. It's about challenging what we consider to be a pathology or disorder by recognizing the different ways we exist and function as diverse humans. I want to finish this subchapter with a part of a poem found on PluralityResource.org:[44]

Plurality is being depathologized as no longer a disorder in and of itself.
Even if it came about as part of a disorder, it is nonetheless a natural and normally occurring variance.
It is now a 'way of being in and relating to the world'.

41 Anthony Temple, 'No more...(cocoons)(labels)(words)'. Accessed 4 September 2022, https://astraeasweb.net/plural/nomore.html
42 Anthony Temple, 'On integration'. Accessed 5 September 2022, www.astraeasweb.net/plural/integrate.html
43 Astraea, 'Defining our experience: Who decides?' Accessed 5 September 2022. http://astraeasweb.net/plural/who-decides.html
44 Plurality Resource, 'V – Our Movement', Plurality Resource: Online Classes for and by Plurals. Accessed 6 September 2022, https://pluralityresource.org/our-movement

It is a strength, it is a gift.
It is not a curse, nor is it a weakness.
It is something we possess and experience.
It does not mean we are any less than those not like us.
It is no longer wrong; it is right for us.'

– Liberty, Serenity *et al.* for Nu Upsilon Xi (NYΞ), The Sorority

Moving forward...

I really hope that reading this chapter has given you the opportunity to notice how so many deficits and traits of so-called disorders are actually just ways that individuals diverge from societal norms and expectations. I hope you have been able to recognize how many of these dominant societal norms and expectations are actually rooted in white supremacy and capitalism as well as how society has created this ideal person with an ideal set of characteristics that has masqueraded as normal. I hope you have been able to see how society labels anyone with a disorder if they don't meet their concept of the ideal person who functions the right way according to society. There are a myriad of ways to feel, to learn, to think, to communicate, to function and to exist, and one way is no more right than other ways. While we may find certain characteristics and traits more beneficial or more difficult depending on the context of our own lives and culture, no characteristic or trait is more right or normal than others. When it comes to neurodiversity and challenging neuronormativity, we need to reject the notion of the right way to function, and we need to reject the notion of an ideal set of characteristics. In fact, we need to reject the notion of normal in general.

CHAPTER 9

A Neurodiversity-Affirming Society

If I had to picture a neurodiversity-affirming society, I would see a society where individuals are no longer pathologized for their differences, needs or distress; where individuals are no longer viewed as broken, unwell or abnormal for their existence; and where individuals are no longer othered for their differences. I picture a society where environments such as workplaces and schools accommodate individuals because they recognize the natural diversity in how individuals exist, learn, feel and think. I believe workplaces and schools will be redesigned to meet the needs of various learning, communicating and thinking styles. I want a future where individuals can function according to how they function; where they have the option to work and learn in environments that suit their needs and differences and where they are no longer measured against each other.

In order for society to become affirming of neurodivergent individuals, there are so many things that need to adjust and adapt. We're talking about the organization and structure of classrooms and universities as well as the expectations, demands and structures of workplaces. When we talk about moving forward with a neurodiversity lens, we are committing to changing and improving our environments rather than changing and improving neurodivergent people. We need to explore how we can improve current systems and structures for neurodivergent folks and how we can adapt environments by providing accommodations. If you're a teacher, education, therapist, employer, employee, I genuinely hope this chapter can provide some new solutions, options, ideas and considerations for making your workplace, school or environment more neurodiversity affirming. I do want to preface this by saying that I do not have all the answers, and this book doesn't have all the answers, but I do believe this is a start and that's all I can ask for. Any kind of paradigm shift or change within society starts with small steps, quiet questions and hopeful ideas, and that's what this book is – a hopeful idea containing considerations, potential solutions to try, questions and what ifs.

I feel there are a lot of questions and concerns when we think about replacing the Pathology Paradigm with the Neurodiversity Paradigm, especially when abolishing psychiatry is often a common objective among many individuals. I mean, it's hard to imagine an alternative system when this current system is so ingrained into the very fabric of society – as if almost everything revolves around psychiatry and the Pathology Paradigm and needing the diagnosis of a disorder. If we want to shift from labelling everyone with a disorder and, instead, recognizing individuals as neurodivergent, how do we still ensure that people get the support and accommodations they need and deserve? How do we stop pathologizing neurodivergent experiences and responses without minimizing people's challenges and distress?

Needs-based system

I don't have all the answers to this because I'm just one person, and the solution is so much bigger than me; it needs a community of individuals, collective work and systemic change. However, I do believe a needs-based system where we don't require a diagnosis or a disorder in order to qualify for support or accommodations is where it's at. If we have a needs-based system, the DSM doesn't reign over our insurance companies, mental health services, disability services or even our schools. Instead of relying on psychometric assessments and questionnaires, we rely on curiosity, understanding and collaborative conversations. Instead of assuming the fault lies within the individual, we consider the wider context. Instead of throwing medication at someone, we ask someone how we can support them and what they may need in the moment – sometimes it is medication, but the most important thing is that we are offering a choice. If we had a needs-based system, we would recognize all access needs as valid human needs where everyone got their needs met – not because there was something to be fixed but because it's just the right thing to do.

I do want to reiterate that it doesn't mean we have to do away with all labels, especially when it is evident that labels have served individuals in different ways, myself included. But what it does mean is this: we don't weaponize these labels to take away someone's rights, autonomy or dignity, and we don't view someone as broken or less than for having a label that differs from others. Basically, we do not have to let a diagnosis be the master of the support we do and do not receive. Can you imagine what it would be like if our society had a needs-based system where all you had to do was state that you're in need and that was enough? Can you imagine asking your boss at work for an accommodation because you needed the support, and they just did it, no questions asked? Can you imagine asking your teacher for a different way to do the assignment because you learn in a different way, and they were happy to accommodate you? Can you imagine receiving all the accommodations and support to help you thrive because that's what you deserve as a human being?

Universal Design for neurodivergence

We shouldn't be retrofitting or adjusting environments when it comes to everyday spaces like workplaces or classrooms; we should be designing spaces and environments with neurodivergent individuals in mind from the get-go. After all, neurodivergent individuals shouldn't be an afterthought even though we so often are. In order to design spaces and environments for all individuals, rather than just some individuals, we need to consider Universal Design. Universal Design refers to the design of physical environments, such as buildings, to be accessible and user-friendly for all people regardless of their ability. Instead of relying on individual accommodations that an employee or a student needs to ask for and often prove with paperwork and forms, Universal Design sets up spaces to meet the needs of every individual. In a way, this removes feeling like a burden, which is how neurodivergent and disabled individuals feel when they ask for accommodations at work or school. Instead of inclusion being offered on a case-by-case basis, inclusion should be built into the workplace or classroom. Instead of inclusion being an afterthought, it should be an integral part of every environment and every space.

While Universal Design focuses on physical access, there is so much more that Universal Design can focus on in regard to accessibility. I'm not just talking about sensory accommodations such as sound and light; I'm also talking about how individuals communicate, process information, pay attention or focus, and even how individuals learn. Whenever we think of accessibility, we also don't think enough about time; we focus on spaces, environments, sensory needs and tangible strategies, but we rarely ever focus on time. As individuals can experience time differently, we need to accommodate this within our society and especially our workplaces and classrooms. In fact, I think we can even accommodate this within our relationships and everyday life, too. It can be as simple as respecting that individuals can take different amounts of time to respond to messages and calls or providing flexibility when it comes to deadlines, meetings and appointments. It can be as simple as not labelling someone as lazy, uncaring or irresponsible if they are late or need to reschedule last minute, as well as respecting that not everyone has the same 24 hours in a day.

We cannot deny that every individual is different with their own unique needs, and sometimes this means individuals can have conflicting needs. Someone may need to seek out sensory input while someone else may need to avoid sensory input, so it begs the question: how on earth can workplaces even accommodate every difference and every need? I think the solution comes down to designing spaces where individuals have a choice, where we empower individuals with the option to meet their specific needs or accommodate their differences. Imagine if workplaces had an area where people can focus alone, an area where they can collaborate with others, an area free from distractions and an area that is stimulating. If we consider sensory differences and the fact that individuals often have conflicting sensory needs, perhaps the solution comes down to designing spaces where individuals can control the sensory input or designing spaces where individuals have options in regard to sensory input.

On the other hand, every individual may focus or pay attention differently, so it's about giving individuals the option to decide how they'll focus best to get the job done. It's also not just the environment that needs to be adjusted or designed with our differences in mind; it's the policies, procedures and processes of workplaces, too. It could be as simple as allowing for different ways that employees can participate in meetings, providing an agenda for upcoming meetings, presenting materials and information in a variety of ways or accepting multiple forms of communication whether it's spoken, written, text or email.

When it comes to designing learning spaces, it's not just the physical aspects of classrooms like seating that need to be designed to accommodate the diversity of our differences; it's also about designing how teaching and learning is done, too. In an article titled 'Disability studies in education: The need for a plurality of perspectives on disability', the authors argue:

> Instead of tediously piecing together accommodations or modifications based on what we believe a learner can or cannot do (should or should not do), we design in ways that offer a spectrum of possibility. We structure our teaching always and already designed for the many ways that learners can engage learning, thus allowing opportunity to emerge in each new moment, in each new day.[1]

We need to recognize that every individual learns differently and expresses their knowledge differently. I'm not so good at expressing my knowledge through spoken communication, but I can definitely express my knowledge through the written word, which is why I'm writing this book instead of creating a podcast or YouTube channel. When I was studying at university, I always found exams and tests overwhelming and difficult, while written assignments like essays were a lot easier for me. As a result, the grades from exams never truly reflected the knowledge I had gained, but written assignments did.

CAST, an organization dedicated to transforming education and learning, has developed a framework for Universal Design for Learning (UDL) that focuses on providing flexibility in how individuals

---

1   Susan Baglieri, Jan W. Valle, David J. Connor and Deborah J. Gallagher, 'Disability studies in education: The need for a plurality of perspectives on disability', *Remedial and Special Education* 32, no. 4 (May 2010): 267–78. https://doi.org/10.1177/0741932510362200

learn as well as how they express their knowledge.[2] UDL is all about providing options: options for communication as well as expression, options for comprehension, options for perception, options for language and symbols, as well as options for regulation and executive functioning. It's about avoiding the one-size-fits-all methods of instruction, teaching and learning, and instead providing flexible options for all types of learners and all types of students. The Center for Teaching and Learning have pointed out some key differences between traditional classrooms and UDL classrooms:[3]

Traditional classrooms	UDL classrooms
Teaching focuses on what is taught.	Teaching focuses on what is taught as well as how it is taught.
Students can access accommodations based on their diagnosis.	Accommodations are for all students regardless of a diagnosis.
Teachers decide on how a topic is taught.	Students decide how they learn best.
Classrooms have a fixed set-up.	Classrooms have a flexible set-ups.
Assignments can be completed in one way.	Assignments can be completed multiple ways.

Universal Design for neurodivergence isn't about accommodating needs on the basis of having a disability or diagnosis; it's about

2   CAST, 'The UDL Guidelines', CAST, 2 September 2022. https://udlguidelines.cast. org
3   Itzel Ortega Mendez, 'Universal design for learning: Fostering neurodiversity, equity, and inclusivity through educational technology', Center for Teaching and Learning, 27 September 2019. https://commons.hostos.cuny.edu/ctl/universal-design-for-learning-fostering-neurodiversity-equity-and-inclusivity-through-educational-technology

recognizing diversity and the multiple ways of existing and functioning in this world where individuals deserve to have their needs met because they are human, not because a piece of paper says so. It's about acknowledging neurodiversity and empowering employees or students to have a choice in how they work, function or learn. Imagine a workplace having various spaces that were designed with people's needs and differences in mind. If individuals need a low-stimulating environment to be able to focus, there could be a specific area with low stimulation. If individuals need more stimulation when working, there could be a specific area that provides stimulation. If individuals need fewer distractions and less socializing, there could be a low-traffic area, and if people need the opposite, such as more movement and more engagement, there could be high-traffic areas. If these spaces and environments were provided within a workplace, each individual could choose where they may prefer to work on a given day, knowing their needs and capacity.

I also believe Universal Design within workplaces and education can reduce the risk of stigma, discrimination and even segregation because these built-in accommodations are available to everyone. It's well known that neurodivergent individuals, especially those with a stigmatized diagnosis, experience stigma, stereotyping and even outright bullying and exclusion. Not only would Universal Design reduce the risk of a neurodivergent individual being targeted or singled out, but it would also mean they wouldn't have to go through that negative and harmful experience. Disclosing our diagnosis, disability or neurodivergence always puts us at risk, either at risk of harm or at risk of being seen differently, which can result in a loss of opportunities. If you're Autistic, you can be denied management positions based on the stereotype that we 'lack people skills'. I mean, just look at the stereotyping that is already happening within workplaces for neurodivergent individuals. Over the past few years, a number of workplaces have created neurodiversity-affirming programmes where Autistic individuals can thrive. Sure, it's nice that they're finally recognizing that Autistic individuals have strengths and just need the right accommodations to thrive within the workplace, but there is a catch. Most of these programmes are computer, technology or analytical based, like data entry, because of the stereotype that all Autistic people are good with computers or numbers. I wanted to bring this up because workplaces are trying to be neurodiversity affirming by creating these programmes for Autistic individuals, but they're not treating us as equal employees or even as individuals with various strengths, skills and interests; they're treating us like a stereotype, like a niche. That's the thing about neurodiversity: we want workplaces to accommodate our differences without forcing us into a box.

I think that is what it all comes down to, you know? I'm merely asking society to respect and accommodate individuals because we are worthy and deserving regardless of label, any diagnosis. I am asking for acceptance and understanding because no one ever deserves to feel terrible about themselves or miss out on opportunities. If we were to move towards a needs-based system, if we were to design spaces with neurodivergent individuals in mind, it may be helpful to explore what different needs look like and how we can accommodate them by adapting and improving our environments.

Adjusting workplaces

I'm not sure if you've noticed but neurodiversity has become all the rage when it comes to workplaces, and not always in a good way. Unfortunately, neurodiversity has become a buzzword within workplaces without workplaces doing the work to understand what neurodiversity means. In fact, often workplaces will say neurodiversity or neurodivergence when really they mean Autistic or ADHD, which ends up in workplaces accommodating or, at least, trying to accommodate Autistic and ADHD individuals, while other neurodivergent individuals and their needs are ignored. As a multiple neurodivergent individual, I need accommodations for all of the ways I am neurodivergent. If you accommodate my Autism, I need you to accommodate my bipolar and manic episodes; there's no picking and choosing what needs or differences you get to accommodate.

While there is a long list of helpful accommodations coming up, there's one accommodation in particular that I wanted to point out because it's an accommodation that every single individual, neurodivergent or otherwise, would benefit from. If there's one way you adjust your workplaces, it needs to be allowing employees to pick and adjust their hours and having the option to work from home. I've had many jobs and I've been in many workplaces, and the workplaces that were most accommodating for me were those that offered the most flexibility in where I worked, when I worked and how I worked. More often than not, it wasn't the job itself that proved to be difficult; it was the environment I was expected to work in, which is why the option to work from home, an environment where I could work because it was set up to accommodate my needs, was so helpful. If you're a workplace and you can't change the environment for whatever bureaucratic reason, you could at least trust your employee enough to choose where they do their job. I cannot begin to express how this flexibility would accommodate so many neurodivergences and so many differences.

○ ○ ○

ACCOMMODATIONS IN WORKPLACES ↓

Accommodations for sensory differences

- Provide white noise machines, sound-absorbing panels and/or wall partitions.

- Allow desks to be relocated to another area as required.

- Allow noise-cancelling headphones, noise-reducing earplugs and sunglasses or tinted glasses.

- Uniforms are not compulsory to accommodate sensory differences.

- Provide a low-stimulus area for individuals with heightened sensory sensitivity.

- Encourage the use of support objects.

- Provide a written summary of any spoken communication.

- Allow virtual attendance and participation for meetings.

- Allow the use of recording devices during meetings and spoken instructions.

Accommodations for social interactions

- Keep the office door closed during focus hours.

- Receive communication through written format (e.g. email instead of phone calls).

- Assign 'Do not disturb' hours.

- Provide a visual sign with instructions on how to interact (e.g. knock before entering).

- Regularly work from home/remote work days.

- Allow non-compulsory attendance at social events

Accommodations for communication differences

- Allow time to process giving answers to questions.

- Do not label direct communication as rude or passive-aggressive.

- Say what you mean without hinting or implying information.

- Do not make assumptions – clarify first.

- Allow the use of a recording device during meetings and verbal instructions.

- Allow time to respond to verbal communication including questions.

- Respect the use of AAC or written communication.

- Provide instructions and materials in multiple forms of communication.

Accommodations for respecting plurality, alters, systems and multiples

- Allow individuals to have a name tag of whoever is fronting.

- Request that colleagues and employers respect names.

- Provide room to adjust the name as needed.

- Accommodate memory issues by providing written communication (paper record).

- Have written instructions on how to complete tasks readily available.

- Provide flexible working hours.

- Assist individuals in filling any gaps in memory if needed.

- Accommodate the need for breaks when switching.

- Allow the use of a recording device during meetings and verbal instructions.

Accommodations for hearing voices or experiencing psychosis

- Allow the ability to leave last minute to accommodate experiences.

- Accommodate absences and remote working.

- Provide a work space where there is lower noise and distraction levels.

- Accommodate individual needs for private work spaces or non-open office plans.

- Create a private space for when individuals may be experiencing hallucinations.

- Allow noise-cancelling headphones, sunglasses or other tools.

- Provide tools that assist with memory recall.

Accommodations for time management and focusing

- Provide a neurodivergent-friendly timer to manage time management on projects/tasks.

- Normalize and utilize fidget items during office hours, including meetings, sessions and sitting at the desk to encourage focus.

- Ensure there are readable clocks around the office.

- Allow for flexible work schedules such as switching from 11-7 rather than 9-5.

- Adjust work schedules to avoid rush hour.

- Allow for staggered focus and task completion rather than eight blocks of focusing.

- Do not view tardiness or lateness as poor attitude.

- Incorporate more breaks.

- Utilize a task flowchart or a checklist.

- Incorporate colour-coded systems such as coloured tabs, folders or sticky notes.

- Divide large tasks into smaller tasks.

- Provide to-do lists with prioritization indicators.

Accommodations for memory

- Provide written summaries of any form of meetings.

- Provide verbal summaries in the form of debriefing after any meetings.

- Provide instructions and deadlines via written communication.

- Streamline methods of communication through one source or app such as email, Slack, etc.

- Provide verbal and written reminders.

Accommodations for organizing, planning and prioritizing

- Provide additional training time to go over new programmes, tasks and instructions.

- Provide colour-coded instructions, manuals, checklists and maps.

- Encourage body doubling and/or the sharing of strengths and skills.

- Divide large tasks into smaller tasks.

- Provide to-do lists with prioritization indicators.

Accommodations for hyperactivity

- Allow the use of fidget items during meetings and work sessions.

- Provide a variety of seating (e.g. office chairs, kneeling chairs, bouncy ball).

- Have alternative workstations including standing desks.

- Modify break schedules (e.g. multiple small breaks).

- Normalize the use of movement during completing tasks, meetings and more.

Accommodations for learning differences

- Offer alternative ways to complete tasks, paperwork or reports.

- Present instructions orally, visually and in written form.

- Provide a glossary of relevant terms.

- Provide grips for pens and pencils.

- Use easy-to-read fonts in all materials.

- Provide materials or written instructions with large print or double spacing.

- Allow the use of text-to-speech or speech-to-text software.

- Highlight important information.

- Provide written and verbal summaries of any meetings.

- Allow extra time for completing projects and tasks.

- Provide written materials with text is that legible and not italicized.

- Provide proofreading and copywriting assistance as needed.

- Utilize colour-contrast overlays to increase legibility of documents.

- Provide instructions verbally, written and visually as well as through demonstration.

**Accommodations for emotional differences
and mood episodes**

- Provide flexible deadlines to accommodate changes
  in mood.

- Provide a space for regular breaks.

- Allow for a flexible work environment, whether it's
  working for home or flexible scheduling.

- Provide natural lighting where possible.

- Provide extended time for projects, KPIs (key
  performance indicators) and tasks.

- Provide a space to retreat to when in emotional distress.

- Allow for unlimited use of the bathroom.

- Allow for shortened work days or starting work
  days later.

Adjusting learning environments

In order to be neurodiversity affirming, we need to accommodate
the way individuals learn as well as how we pay attention, how we
regulate and how we communicate. It's about honouring and respecting the differences and needs of all students by creating environments where they can thrive, because when students thrive, they
will learn so much more easily. As it is, the traditional education
system in our society, as many neurodivergent individuals and parents are aware, doesn't actually cater for our learning differences.
let alone all the other ways that we are different.

If you're a parent reading this, I want you to know that some-times traditional school isn't always the right fit and it isn't always the only option. I've been following a number of neurodivergent parents of neurodivergent kids; through them, I have discovered alternatives to traditional schooling and one of them is self-directed education. Ann Hansen, a developmental specialist and unschooling advocate, shares on Instagram that self-directed edu-cation 'is simply learning without coercion'.[4] What Ann means by this is that all learning is done from life experiences and activities that children choose. What stands out for me is that every child is supported and encouraged to follow their interests and curiosity, and if you're wondering, self-directed education doesn't mean you can't follow a structured curriculum; it's just up to the child to want that because, as Ann shares, 'it is the child who is guiding the expe-rience. It is their choice so they are typically more invested'.[5] That's the wonderful thing about self-directed education: children can follow their passions and engage with a topic deeply if they wish, free from the time restraints and constraints of a traditional class-room. I also think a significant part of what makes self-directed education a neurodiversity-affirming option is that it honours and respects how neurodivergent children may develop according to their unique timeline. Instead of forcing children to reach predeter-mined developmental and learning milestones that fail to account for a child's differences, self-directed education allows children to choose what they learn and how they learn, which means they can play, behave, learn and communicate in a way that works for them. While traditional education encourages only certain forms of learn-ing, self-directed education supports each individual in how they

---

4   Ann Hansen (@innerparentcoaching). 'What is self-directed education?' Insta-gram, 2 June 2022. www.instagram.com/p/CeRlxC1Px2u
5   Ann Hansen (@innerparentcoaching), 'What is self-directed education?' Insta-gram, 2 June 2022. www.instagram.com/p/CeRlxC1Px2u

learn best. While traditional education focuses on comparison and competition, self-directed education encourages diversity.

Honestly, traditional education settings such as classrooms could take a page or two out of their book. I wonder what classrooms could look like if teachers were there to support a student's curiosity or self-directed learning instead of instructing according to a rigid curriculum and timeline. I wonder what classrooms could look like if there was more room for play and movement over having to sit at a desk while staring at the whiteboard. Teva, the @neurocurioustherapist on Instagram, says:

> Much of the challenging behaviour we see in schools is caused by the environment. Some kids are deeply affected by the visual, sound, and social structures of school. The constant demands, the bright lights, the cluttered and colourful rooms... The minimal movement, the almost non-existent autonomy, the humiliation of learning differences, the pressure of assessments, the peers who exclude...[6]

If we truly wanted to support neurodivergent students, we would eliminate standardized testing, have way more recesses and breaks, encourage more movement outside of the classroom, get rid of expected attendance and get rid of homework. Dr Naomi Fisher says:

> Most adults know that their psychological wellbeing is improved when they can make meaningful choices in their life, when they are not afraid or shamed and when they are not constantly comparing

---

6   Teva (@neurocurioustherapist), 'Much of the challenging behaviour we see in schools is caused by the environment', Instagram, 10 September 2022. www.instagram.com/p/CiTEKVovluJ

themselves against others. We seem to forget that the same principles apply to young people.[7]

While Dr Naomi Fisher wasn't necessarily talking about neurodivergent individuals, this absolutely applies to neurodivergent individuals. If schools were set up to support how each student learns
differently and shares knowledge differently, everyone could play
to their strengths. If schools didn't focus so much on grading, attendance and standardized testing, students would stop comparing themselves to each other. If schools didn't focus on punishments and rewards in so many aspects of their classrooms, students
would be less afraid. If we truly wanted to support neurodivergent
students, we would offer alternative learning environments as well
as entirely different education options.

I genuinely both hope and believe the above recommendations
can become a norm in our society. I know the unschooling advocates, self-directed learning advocates and neurodivergent parents
who choose to home-school will pave the way in spreading awareness, creating home-schooling communities and models or even
just by showing that another way is possible. I mean, if I hadn't followed these advocates and parents, I wouldn't even have known
this was an option or a possibility. While I recognize that we cannot
dismantle and rebuild our education system in a day or even a dec-
ade, perhaps changing our education system will be like a game of
Jenga: removing a block at a time until we can replace the holes
with something new, something better. In the meantime, we can
do our best to accommodate all the differences with the resources

7   Naomi Fisher, 'The side effects of school: A crisis in mental health can't be solved
through therapy', Progressive Education, 17 April 2022. www.progressiveeducation.
org/the-side-effects-of-school-a-crisis-in-mental-health-cant-be-solved-through-
therapy-by-dr-naomi-fisher

we've got, while advocating for more resources, more money and more progress.

ACCOMMODATIONS IN EDUCATIONAL SETTINGS ⬇

Accommodations for managing sensory differences

- Allow the use of noise-cancelling headphones.

- Allow students to listen to music while completing schoolwork.

- Incorporate sound-absorbing panels to reduce outside noise.

- Allow the use of noise-reducing earplugs that reduce the intensity of sounds.

- Allow students to make their uniforms more sensory friendly.

- Allow the use of sunglasses or tinted glasses while in the classroom.

- Provide a low-stimulus study area for individuals with sensory differences.

- Allow the presence of a support animal or support objects.

- Provide grips for pens and pencils.

- Utilize a range of seating options (e.g. beanbags, swivel chairs, floor seating).

- Allow for unlimited use of the bathroom.

Accommodations for social differences

- Do not enforce social interactions during recess, lunch or breaks.

- Create visual signs for when individuals aren't in a socializing mood.

- Provide visual signage with instructions on how to interact (e.g. ask before engaging).

- Allow non-compulsory attendance to social events such as school formals.

- Do not punish lack of attendance.

Accommodations for communication differences

- Allow time to process giving answers to questions.

- Provide ample preparation time for pop quizzes – remove the 'pop' from pop quizzes.

- Do not label direct communication as rude or passive-aggressive.

- Say what you mean without hinting or implying information.

- Do not make assumptions – clarify first.

- Allow the use of a recording device.

- Allow time to respond to verbal communication including questions.

- Respect the use of AAC or written communication.

- Provide instructions and teaching in multiple forms of communication.

- Allow assignments to be completed in multiple ways.

Accommodations for respecting plurality, alters, systems and multiples

- Provide a space for individuals to ground themselves as needed.

- Have access to rules, expectations or instructions that is in verbal as well as written format.

- Allow for extra time for tests, exams and quizzes to accommodate switching or dissociation.

- Provide content warnings for triggers and highly sensitive topics to allow students to leave the classroom if they might be triggered.

- Provide tools that assist with memory recall.

- Respect and honour the name of who is fronting.

Accommodations for hearing voices and psychosis

- Allow individuals to remove themselves from a situation.

- Accommodate absences and remote learning.

- Provide a space where there is lower noise and distraction levels.

- Create a private space for when individuals may be experiencing hallucinations.

- Allow noise-cancelling headphones, sunglasses or other tools.

- Offer alternative curriculum when certain topics are distressing or triggering.

- Allow extra time to complete assignments, tests or exams.

- Provide tools that assist with memory recall.

Accommodations for time management and focusing

- Provide a neurodivergent-friendly timer to manage time management on projects/tasks.

- Normalize and utilize fidget items.

- Ensure there are readable clocks around the classroom.

- Allow for staggered focus and task completion rather than eight blocks of focusing.

- Do not view tardiness or lateness as poor attitude.

- Incorporate more breaks, including movement breaks.

- Utilize a task flowchart or a checklist with visual and written reminders.

- Incorporate a colour-coded system such as coloured tabs, folders or sticky notes.

- Divide large tasks into smaller tasks.

- Provide to-do lists with prioritization indicators.

Accommodations for memory difficulties

- Provide written summaries of previous classes.

- Provide instructions and deadlines via written communication so we can check back on it.

- Provide verbal and written reminders.

- Break down steps and instructions.

- Present concepts and topics in a variety of different ways.

- Provide flowcharts for procedures, activities and assignments.

- Avoid open-ended questions and pop quizzes.

Accommodations for hyperactivity

- Allow the use of fidget items.

- Provide a variety of seating (e.g. wiggle chairs, kneeling chairs, exercise balls, bean bags).

- Provide alternative learning spaces such as standing desks.

- Modify break schedules with multiple small breaks.

- Normalize the use of movement.

- Allow space to complete assignments or take tests where students can move freely.

- Teach topics in alternative formats such as physical activities or practical activities.

- Allow for unlimited use of the bathroom.

Accommodations for learning differences

- Use a variety of teaching styles and methods.

- Provide computer-assisted learning or hands-on activities.

- Offer alternative ways to complete assignments, homework or tests.

- Present instructions orally, visually and in written form.

- Provide a glossary of relevant content terms.

- Allow understanding to be demonstrated in different ways.

- Provide grips for pens and pencils.

- Don't grade homework or tasks based on handwriting or spelling.

- Provide handouts or written instructions with large print or double spacing.

- Allow the use of text-to-speech or speech-to-text software.

- Provide access to audiobooks if textbooks are needed.

- Allow use of a calculator or cheat sheet with formulas.

Accommodations for managing emotional differences and mood episodes

- Provide the opportunity to learn from home to accommodate mood changes.

- Ensure classrooms have visible reminders to eat, drink, rest and take a break.

- Provide natural lighting where possible.

- Provide extended time for assignments and tests.

- Provide a space to retreat to when in emotional distress.

- Allow for unlimited use of the bathroom.

- Allow for shortened school days.

Adjusting your lifestyle and home

While it is so important to focus on adjusting workplaces and class-rooms to accommodate neurodivergent individuals, we sometimes forget that we also need to adjust our lifestyle and home. Our home should be our safe space – the one space where we don't have to mask, pretend or ignore our needs. And for neurodivergent children, home should be the one place where they can unmask, be them-selves and have their needs met because, so often, classrooms are exhausting and overwhelming because they aren't accommodating.

If our home is an affirming environment, it also gives us a chance to rest and recharge before stepping back out into a neurotypical world. I've lived in homes that weren't so affirming, and as a child and teenager, my own home wasn't affirming. I don't blame my par-ents; they didn't have access to affirming resources or support like we do today. I mean, I've only just figured out how to make my own home meet my needs, and I'm the one living with my needs, so I can't imagine how difficult it would have been to figure out how to meet my needs when I could barely communicate them as a child. Anyway, it's allowed me to realize what a significant difference having an affirming home and lifestyle can make when it comes to being neurodivergent.

I want to share an example of the difference it can make, using my own lived experience. I used to live by myself while working part-time and studying full-time, and it wasn't sustainable at all, especially because I didn't accommodate my differences or needs at home, at university or at work. I was constantly exhausted, constantly in sensory overload, constantly irritable, constantly on the verge of meltdowns, and I wasn't managing life at all. I skipped a lot of classes, and if I wasn't calling in sick to work, I would be changing jobs after six months. I would forget bills and appointments, and I would always have dishes piling up. I would have unwashed clothes sitting in the laundry till even washing them wouldn't make a difference. I rarely put my clothes away, which meant I had a magnificent floor-drobe, and my sleeping made attending morning classes, work shifts and appointments extremely difficult. It's probably only been in the last few years that I've been able to make adjustments in my life and put accommodations in place in my home. If there's one adjustment that has made the biggest impact, it would be no longer working full-time or even part-time. I admit, it is a privilege that I've been able to find a form of income through advocacy and writing that is flexible and predominantly online, but I think it's an accommodation that everyone deserves. I don't live alone anymore, either; I live in a shared house, which means housework and sometimes the cooking is shared among us – and, as another bonus, we play to our strengths and needs. I struggle to do the dishes because it's sensory hell with all the gross textures, so another housemate takes care of the dishes. You might be impressed that my clothes actually live in my wardrobe now, and it's all because I have an open wardrobe without any doors or drawers.

See, for me, if something is out of sight behind closed doors, I'm less likely to see it or remember it, and the same goes for doing things: if there's an extra step of having to open the drawer or door, I'm less likely to put my clothes away and more likely to leave them on the floor.

If you're neurodivergent, you've probably had a planner recommended as a way to be organized, and if you're anything like me, you've tried and failed to use calendars and planners. In fact, you probably have a whole drawer full of old planners that you bought with every intention to use, but you lost interest or motivation after a few weeks. I find a planner is another tool simply not suited for a lot of neurodivergent folks. As an alternative, I use a visual planner pad and a wall planner – this is like a planner but there's no flicking through the planner to find the right page, which, trust me, is a barrier to using a planner. I also use visual reminders and put them absolutely everywhere; I'm talking about sticky notes and written lists on my fridge, on my mirror, on my bedroom wall and even on my computer screen. I put them wherever I'm going to see them without having to actually find them. I guess a lot of the ways I make adjustments at home is by finding shortcuts and making everything as easy as possible for me – like the simplest way to get my three meals a day (frozen/pre-cut vegetables) or even the easiest way to brush my teeth (hint: it's an electric toothbrush or toothpaste tablets I can chew). I won't lie, I still struggle to brush my teeth every night, I don't always get my three meals a day, and sometimes I rely on takeaway food because that's the easiest way. But I'm still doing way better and way more than when I was without these adjustments and accommodations.

I used to never spend time in my bedroom in all the places I've lived because my bedroom would just do nothing for me; it was merely a place for sleeping, not hanging out or relaxing. As it turns out, I just needed to make my bedroom a place I actually wanted to spend time in; I needed to make my bedroom a sensory-friendly space if I wanted to find it relaxing. I have a unique set of sensory differences (just like everyone else) where I experience hyposensitivity with some senses and hypersensitivity with others. I tend to fill my bedroom with bright colours, candles with my favourite smells, soft toys, my special interests, pillows and soft lighting. I've even made sure that the blankets on my bed are the right texture as well as the right weight that provides me with just enough pressure to help me sleep. Even if you don't see yourself as having any specific sensory differences, it can still be helpful to turn your bedroom or any space into a sensory space. It can be helpful with relaxing, regulating, reducing distress as well as meeting your sensory needs, whether it's decreasing sensory input or seeking sensory input. I can't imagine anyone who wouldn't benefit from a room that makes them feel calm, safe and good.

I also believe a lot of it comes down to adjusting our expectations as well as redefining what success, functioning, well-being and even independence looks like for us. Maybe full independence where you live alone doesn't have to be the standard or goal; maybe there's nothing wrong with living with friends, housemates, a carer, caregivers or even needing to rely on your partner. Maybe we need to let go of the expectation that we have to stay on top of housework and cooking while working, studying or taking care of a family and, for many people, while doing all three. I believe no one is independent; everyone is actually interdependent. We all rely on support, whether it's someone taking care of our children, fixing our plumbing, driving us somewhere or doing our finances. We all rely on other people to meet our needs such as social needs or emotional needs. The difference is that only some needs and dependencies have been normalized. As discussed in Chapter 8, independence is very much a Western and capitalist ideal and standard.

I think it's also important to acknowledge that there is nothing wrong with not being able to do certain things. In fact, having strengths and weaknesses is just a part of being human rather than an indication that there's something wrong with us. If I can't do certain chores or house duties, I can either find a way to make it easier or I can just accept that it's something I can't do and focus on the things that I can do. This is why we need to allow individuals to define what success looks like for them because success is subjective; it's unique for each individual. In order to adjust our lifestyle and home, we need to understand our differences, recognize our needs and identify barriers, challenges and solutions. In order to make this a little easier (I hope), I've created a small list of prompts to help you reflect on how you can adjust your lifestyle and home.

○ ○ ○

PROMPTS FOR ADJUSTING YOUR HOME AND LIFESTYLE ⬇

- Can you identify any times or situations where your communication needs change (e.g. preferring written methods to communicate)?

- Can you identify which of your senses are hypersensitive and which are hyposensitive?

- Can you list ways you could adjust your home or bedroom to suit your sensory needs?

- Can you identify what chores or household tasks you can find difficult or challenging? It might be helpful to think which chores you avoid the most and explore the reason behind it.

- Can you identify ways you can make these chores or

tasks easier for you? Are there any tools, adjustments or strategies? If it's not possible to make something easier, that's totally fine because we don't have to do everything – we can accept we can't do something.

- Can you incorporate visual reminders, instructions and cues around the house?

- Are there any chores or household tasks that you can break down into steps or use visual cues?

- Can you identify ways that you can accommodate your sensory and executive functioning differences when it comes to cooking and eating?

- Are there any demands or responsibilities that you can outsource or body-double with?

- Are there any sustainable ways that your partner can support you?

- Are there any sustainable ways that your parents, caregiver or carer can support you?

- Are there any sustainable ways that your housemates can support you?

A neurodiversity-affirming future

If we want to be inclusive of all neurodivergent individuals, we need to challenge neuronormativity and we need to accommodate all differences, all needs, all the ways that individuals diverge. I believe the only way we can move towards a neurodiversity-affirming future is by acknowledging the myriad ways that people function, think, learn, communicate, feel, socialize and exist. If there are so many different ways of functioning, existing and doing things, how can certain ways be wrong or abnormal? If we can make more room for all the different ways of functioning within our environments, it means people will have the space to function according to how they function, and maybe, just maybe, people will experience fewer challenges because they have that space, that freedom.

I'll never be able to pay attention in a way that workplaces demand of me, and because workplaces demand that things are done a certain way - their way - it means I struggle to do things. The thing is, though, it doesn't mean I can't do the things. I can absolutely do the things, but I need to be able to do them my way, and while it may look different and may take longer, I'm still doing it. It's the same thing with classrooms. I have always struggled with sitting in a classroom for long periods of time; I would avoid doing my work, I would read instead of listening to the teacher, I would have meltdowns and I wouldn't complete assignments or homework. I would also run away frequently, and the place I would escape to was the library. I wasn't running away to avoid doing work or because I wanted to do something more fun; I would run away to the library because it was a better environment than the classroom. I was looking after my own needs. This doesn't mean I can't learn; it just means that the expectations and rules within classrooms don't work for me - they don't accommodate how I learn, think or communicate. I can learn but I'm not going to learn if I'm sitting still in a classroom while trying to pay attention to the teacher talking at the front of the room. If we can acknowledge that there are multiple ways of doing things instead of one right way to do things, we can move away from trying to fix or change people and we can start moving towards changing and improving society and our systems within society.

If we want to move towards a neurodiversity-affirming society where we are inclusive of all neurodivergent individuals, we also need to acknowledge and dismantle white supremacy culture. White supremacy culture reinforces neuronormativity with standards and expectations that harm us all and it reinforces the belief that there is one right way, which means we cannot make room for all the ways if we don't dismantle white supremacy. White supremacy culture reinforces the expectation that we must be perfect, which puts unfair expectations on people and harms people who cannot meet this unrealistic standard of perfection. White supremacy culture continues to define success and productivity for us. White supremacy culture teaches us to blame our distress on ourselves rather than look at our external environments, systems and society. White supremacy culture reinforces a society where individuals are expected to make it on their own without support, which means that accommodations and support are seen as a burden and even as something someone must earn. White supremacy culture makes us believe that we must do everything ourselves, but community is the answer – community is the solution. And it is white supremacy culture that reinforces binaries of existing, and we cannot make room for all of the ways we function and exist if we do not dismantle white supremacy.

I think it is possible to make room for all the ways we function and exist. I have to hope it's possible, so we can begin to recognize the diversity of functioning. I do know that it is going to take all of us. It will require us to disrupt white supremacy, neuronormativity, heteronormativity and cisnormativity, and challenge ableism, racism and sanism. It will require us to recognize the importance and value of community care, and to abolish old systems to make room for new systems that meet our needs instead of oppressing our differences. I believe a neurodiversity-affirming society will benefit everyone, not just neurodivergent individuals, because we all have differences and needs, and we all function differently whether it's feeling, thinking, socializing, communicating or learning because that's simply neurodiversity. If we can recognize the diversity of functioning, we can create a society where everyone thrives, where everyone has their needs met, where everyone is welcome and, most importantly, where everyone can live their life embracing their differences without feeling that they're a broken human. If we can embrace neurodiversity and challenge neuronormativity, we can stop pathologizing people's differences, challenges and distress.

If you're reading this and you're neurodivergent, I want you to know that your needs and your differences are not a burden, that your distress or suffering doesn't mean there is something wrong with you. I want you to know that you are not less of a person if you need to live with other people, and that you are no less worthy if you cannot work or if you need to work less. I want you to know that you can create your own rules within your relationships. I want you to know that you do not have to be productive all the time, and your productivity can look different to someone else's productivity. In fact, I want you to know that you do not have to be productive to be a valuable member of society. You deserve to have your differences and needs met within workplaces and classrooms. You deserve to design a life according to your own values, definitions, needs and differences.